EXPERIENCE the Living GOD

To God Be the Glory

Lily Liu Wong

ISBN 978-1-0980-0061-5 (paperback)
ISBN 978-1-0980-0062-2 (digital)

Christian Faith Publishing, Inc.
832 Park Avenue
Meadville, PA 16335
www.christianfaithpublishing.com

All scripture references are from the New International Version, except where otherwise noted.

Printed in the United States of America

My special thanks to

Pastor Morris
Janet Deeg
Lou Franklin

and

all my sisters and brothers around the world who give themselves week after week in serving God and others in Bible Study Fellowship.

CONTENTS

PREFACE

> Jesus looked at them and said, "With man, this is impossible, but with God, all things are possible."
>
> —Matthew 19:26

Twice my dear Bible Study Fellowship International (BSF) sister, Kathy Foster, told me that I need to write down all my testimonies that I shared with her over the years. The first time she mentioned it to me several years ago, I didn't pay attention to what she was saying. I just dismissed her words. I was busy with a very tight daily schedule. I knew that writing a book was impossible for me with all that I had going on so I did not go to the Lord about it.

Early in 2017, she reminded me again that I needed to write down all the testimonies that God let me experience during my life. This time, I took her seriously. I went to the Lord and prayed about it. I had many reasons not to do a project such as what Kathy suggested. I was very busy, I was not a writer, and I didn't know how to start such a thing! Writing my testimonies would be an enormous task. When the Lord told me to do so, I knew that I need the help of the Holy Spirit in order to do something so impossible.

My friend Kathy mailed me a gift, a picture frame with the following two scriptures written on it:

- "The lot is cast in the lap, but its every decision is from the Lord" (Prov. 16:33).
- "Give thanks to the Lord, for he is good; his love endures forever" (Ps. 107:1).

How the word of God encouraged me. It also confirmed that I needed to take action and write down my many testimonies. So I started in the summer of 2017. With the Holy Spirit as my director, I finished the later stages of my exciting and blessed life. It was more difficult to write about the earlier periods. Through my sister Gladis' love, encouragement, and hospitality during my visits, I finished this difficult project.

- "Give praise to the Lord, proclaim his name; make known among the nations what he has done" (Ps. 105:1).
- "Now to him who is able to do immeasurably more than we ask or imagine, according to his power that is at work within us, to him be glory in the church and in Christ Jesus throughout all generations, for ever and ever! Amen" (Eph. 3:20–21).

Let us experience the living God in so many, many ways as we explore what he has done in my life.

Love,
Lily

1

From the Beginning

My mother, Mary Xiu Zheng Jiang Liu, was a bold Chinese saint of God. A small woman less than five feet tall, her faith was as big as heaven. Every day over the course of her lifetime as she experienced change in her careers, countries, cultures, and centuries, her faith in Jesus was steadfast. She impacted our family's life. Mom raised us to love and obey the Lord. She grew up during a time when it was difficult and dangerous to be a Chinese Christian, especially for a woman. But as a Christian who lived her faith, she feared no man. Serving God was the standard in our family. She expected the same from her children and she raised us to become strong men and women who served the Lord. Through deed, word, and action, Mom was the epitome of a godly woman. We saw Jesus when we looked at our mother. Everyone else did as well.

Ecclesiastes 7:1 says, "A good name is better than fine perfume, and the day of death better than the day of birth." My mom went back to her heavenly home on January 3, 2015. On the first anniversary of her death (2016), I was to serve as the pianist at Southern Oklahoma Chinese Baptist Church (SOCBC) during Sunday worship service. Every time I played the piano, I thought of her. It was her encouragement that led me become a piano teacher and performer. On this anniversary, I arrived at church ready to honor my mom with the talent she saw and encouraged in me.

I wanted it to be a celebratory tribute for the amazing life she lived and serving the God she loved. It was very hard to describe the influence she had on my life. Not only did she pray for me every day of my life, but she was also an amazing example of Christianity. I loved my wonderful mom so dearly. Joy for her influence over my life bloomed in my heart. But as I touched the piano and played the first chord, I began weeping. Like a river flowing out of a dam, it was impossible to stop the tears that flooded down my face. I could no longer see the keyboard, nonetheless I continued to play. I did not understand what was happening to me. I never lost control of my emotions like this. My faithful Lord responded quickly to my confusion. I heard his soft, sweet, and loving voice, "Today is a divine appointment, a remembrance of your mom's will for me." Immediately, my tears stopped. Yes, I would honor my mother's devotion to God. Elation overwhelmed me. My fingers kept playing and my heart rejoiced!

My mother's walk with God started very early. In the Chinese culture, the matriarch plays a very important role in the family. My mother's elderly aunt was such a person. When my mom was a little girl, her aunt visited her house and began discussing idols and how our family must know the truth about them.

> *But their idols are silver and gold, made by human hands. They have mouths, but cannot speak, eyes, but cannot see. They have ears, but cannot hear, noses, but cannot smell. They have hands, but cannot feel, feet, but cannot walk, nor can they utter a sound with their throats. Those who make them will be like them, and so will all who trust in them.* (Psalm 115:4–8)

My mother paid very close attention to what she had heard from her aunt. She was very curious about it even though she didn't really understand everything that been discussed. As she grew older, Mom decided to find the truth about these idols herself. She went to explore Mount Lau, a sacred mountain for the Taoist religion. There she found the idols that her aunt told her about. At first they frightened her because they were so daunting. She saw these huge statues of false gods, some of them were standing and some were seated. They were hideous looking. They had eyes, ears, hands, feet, and mouths but they could not see, hear, feel, walk, or eat. Although they were extremely imposing, there was absolutely no breath in them. She also saw the idols called earth gods on the side of the road. Mom was told that they had to be repaired by human hands after heavy rains or storms. *People had to fix them?* Her fear receded. In her heart, she saw the truth that those frightening looking idols were man-made. They could not even withstand normal, everyday storms but had to be repaired by people. The man-made idols were not the true god. My mother knew that they were lies. Not only had she heard about them from her elderly aunt, she observed them for herself. She understood that what the old aunt told her family was the truth.

In 1937, Japan invaded China and war broke out. In an act of desperation, my grandmother sent her daughters to a church for sanctuary and refuge. They sought protection from the invasion of the Japanese soldiers. It was a time of tension and uncertainty. Although Americans hear John 3:16 all of the time, it was not well-known in China. My mother and her sister, while hiding in the church, heard the beloved scripture for the first time in their lives. "For God so loved the world that he gave his one and only Son that whoever believes in him shall not perish but have eternal life" (John 3:16).

Mom met Jesus while hiding in this church from the Japanese during World War II. The beautiful praise music softened her heart and the weekly sermons filled her with the truth of Christ through God's word. At the age of eighteen, she became a believer. From that day on, she built an intimate and loving relationship with her heavenly Father. In the midst of war grew the seeds of a powerful prayer warrior in Mary Jiang. My mother also fell in love with the piano. It brought her such comfort as she was in hiding from the enemy. She listened to it hour after hour as the church musician performed. She vowed to God that if she had children, she would see that they would serve him with that beautiful instrument.

2

Growing Up

In addition to meeting Jesus while hiding in that old church, she also met an older man whose younger brother needed a wife. This gentleman was so impressed by Mom's beauty, intelligence, and faith that he brought his brother, a pharmacist, to meet my mom. A marriage was arranged, and my parents were married in 1946.

Both my brother Jack and sister Grace were born in China. Father worked at the United Nations Relief and Rehabilitation Administration as a high-ranking officer, which put the Liu family in danger. When the Chinese Communists Revolution began in 1949, an arrest warrant was issued for my father because he worked for the UN. He would have been persecuted and most likely executed had he not taken my mother's advice to flee immediately to Taiwan. A close relative obtained passage on a ship for my parents, brother, sister, and an uncle to escape mainland China. They did not even get a chance to say goodbye to their families. Their departure was sudden and very secret. With just one day's notice, they sailed from Qingdao to Taiwan. They left so quickly that they were ill-equipped for the long journey, but because my brother Jack reminded the captain of his own small grandson, he looked after my family. Under the skipper's protection, the Lord kept all of them alive and well. When they reached Taiwan, they knew no one and had nothing. They were strangers in their new land. They left all their relatives and acquaintances in China and had to start completely over with a new life—at least they were alive.

After being in Taiwan for a while, my dad was walking down the street in Taipei when he ran into an old classmate from Qilu University of Technology, the most famous university in China. Dad mentioned that he desperately needed a job so that he could provide for his family. The classmate recommended my father to a government organization called The Joint Commission on Rural Reconstruction. It was a high-profile job with a good salary. By the grace of God, my dad was hired. My parents finally were able to settle down and establish a home in safety. The income was not a lot, but God provided for the family's needs.

Mom and Dad walked away from everything they had in China, but their one splurge was music. Mom adored Chinese opera. Each Wednesday evening, my father took her to the auditorium of the National Taiwan Normal University, which was only one street from our home. They never missed walking to the university to listen to the Beijing Opera performance live every week. When Mom discovered that she was pregnant with me, they continued to attend the opera so that I was exposed to beautiful music even while in my mother's womb. Naturally, I have loved music all my life. When I was born in 1950, my father had hoped for a second son instead of a second daughter. Although he was very disappointed initially, he eventually grew to love me as I did him. Afterward, my younger brother James and two younger sisters, Gloria and Gladis, were born. We grew into a family of six children. That was quite a challenge for a family starting over in a new place but we had an advantage being a family whose bedrock was Christ.

Mom and Dad loved God. They belonged to the local church. Dad was one of twelve elders; Mom was one of two female deacons. When they bought their home, they immediately offered it up as a family church for the body of Christ in Taipei. Number 14, our home, was dedicated for the Lord's use. For more than ten years, we praised, prayed, and had the Lord's Supper every Sunday night in our home. It was a home full of love. Although both my parents were believers, my mother was definitely the stronger spiritual influence in my life. She expected all of us to serve the Lord and to help those around us. With her love for God displayed constantly in our home life, my siblings and I grew up in the church. Mom raised all six of us children just as Deuteronomy 11:19 instructed, "Teach them to your children, talking about them when you sit at home, and when you walk along the road, when you lie down and when you get up." Each day before we ate at the table, she taught us to pray to God one by one. "Give thanks to God," she would say. She also helped us memorize Bible verses. To this very day, my brothers and sisters can quote scriptures and we are comforted by the words of God that we learned as kids at our parents' table.

Mom worked outside the home as a volunteer nurse at Gospel Clinic of Taipei for more than ten years. It was owned by our local church. She worked with godly doctors who treated the physical as well as the spiritual needs of the patients. Because of Mom's spiritual wisdom, the doctors would ask her to join them as they knelt and prayed asking for God's guidance. During this prayer time, they would discern how to treat some of their most difficult patients. Mom learned how to solve impossible cases. Always, the medical team gave God the glory for healing. Later when I began practicing acupuncture, Mom shared a great deal of the knowledge and insight that she acquired during these prayer times. She also taught me the same basic principles that she and the Christian doctors used—go to the Lord with thanksgiving then ask for his direction and wisdom when helping patients.

Both of my parents practiced hospitality as a ministry and reached out to college students who were far from home and feeling lonely. My parents took care of overseas students from the Philippines, Indonesia, Singapore, Malaysia, and Hong Kong. They especially welcomed those from Vietnam. Because of the Vietnam War, these students couldn't go home during the school breaks so they gathered at our house. The Vietnamese students would spend years in Taiwan before they could go back home. My parents acted as surrogates for the homesick scholars, filling in for their parents as unto the Lord. Besides giving out great love, acceptance, and emotional support, Mom and Dad would send us kids to deliver home-cooked meals or "love feasts" to their dormitories in the middle of the week to ensure that these beloved students would not get hungry. When they became ill, Mom took care of them and nursed them through their illnesses while Dad obtained medication for them. Mom and Dad even let the students stay in our home. They experienced what the love of Jesus was through my parents' example. This practical love established the groundwork for these young people to come to Christ. My mother prayed the Sinner's Prayer with many college students. It was a wonderful way to spread the gospel. These students would take their newly discovered faith back to their home countries where they in turn led their friends and families to Jesus. Our family impacted the world with a Christian love manifested through practical actions surrounded by prayer.

Music was also prevalent in our home. Mom remembered her promise to God that she made in that old church during the war. Because music had comforted her soul during that horrible time, she vowed that she would provide piano lessons for her children. When I was six years old, Mom started looking for a piano teacher for me. Since Taiwan is a small island, whenever she heard the sound of a piano, she would listen, go find the house from where the music was coming, and then knock at the door to inquire who their teacher was. She walked up and down through the many alleys of Taipei, listening for the sound of pianos to find the best piano teacher for her children. All four of us girls took piano lessons. One day, my mother decided to change our piano teacher. She chose a teacher who was also a piano student at National Taiwan Normal University (NTNU). We were under strict training. We all had to spend time practicing the piano, which I enjoyed playing more than any of my sisters. I delighted in my time at the keys. The teacher told Mom that I was the one with the most talent at the piano. With my mother determined that I would make the most of my gift, I received serious discipline from her whenever I was uncooperative. Not only was it the Chinese way, it was also the way things were handled by that generation of parents. If I skipped a daily practice session, I was punished so harshly that I would feel bruised. Despite that discipline, through the mercy and grace of God, I fell in love with the piano and had a passion in my soul for music.

I was fifteen when I started serving the Lord as a pianist for Sunday worship. This is when I learned the skill of sight reading. Sight reading is playing a musical piece just by looking at it the first time without any practice. I played whatever hymns the minister would select in that moment at every service. It was good training for me. When I graduated from high school in 1968, I was accepted as a piano major at NTNU, the best music university in Taiwan. I was privileged to study with the famous piano professor, Dr. Robert Sholz, an internationally known exchange professor from the United States. I learned a lot from him as my skills grew. I played more difficult pieces with better technique. At the very first concert to feature the most gifted young Taiwanese, I was blessed to be selected as one of the pianists. It was an honor and a joy to share my gift with so many people. I loved it. Despite her tough ways, I am grateful to my mother for instilling in me the discipline necessary to becoming a top-tier pianist. My gift, of course, is from God Almighty, and to him goes all glory. Mom just kept me plugged in to make the most of the potential He provided.

While I was at the university, I increased my practice time. Every free possible moment, I gave over to the piano. I played hours at a time but it wasn't enough for me. I wanted to spend even more time growing my skill. But I soon paid a physical price for my obsession. One evening after many hours of practicing, my lower back began to spasm. The pain was the most severe that I had ever experienced. It hurt so badly that I couldn't even stand up. I was so frightened! I couldn't move at all, as if I was paralyzed! My dad, who was now working as a the head of the pharmaceutical department for the US Naval Medical Research Center told me that Chinese acupuncture would work for me to alleviate my symptoms. I had no other choice. I couldn't even walk to my bed! He inserted two needles in the back of my knees. It was like fire. I had to bite my lips to keep from screaming.

"This is the cure for my back?" I groaned to myself. "More like an old method of Chinese torture." Tears poured down my cheeks. I was in agony. However, twenty minutes after the needles were pulled out, all of the pain was gone. It was as if nothing had ever been wrong with me! I could walk and move however I wanted. I was healed. It was miraculous!

My grandfather had been a physician in China, which was how my father knew the technique. Plus, Dad had been a medical student at Qilu University. However, because of the eight-year war between Japan and China, his medical school closed so he had to change his major to pharmacy in order to earn a degree. After experiencing the healing in my back from his use of needles, I decided to learn Chinese acupuncture. My parents also decided to expand their knowledge so the three of us all registered at the Taipei Medical School in Acupuncture Healing. We studied Chinese acupuncture together, went to classes together, and did our internships together. We also had some very lively discussions as we studied and practiced our homework together! After two years of stringent study, Mom, Dad, and I graduated as licensed Chinese acupuncturists. I'm so thankful for this accomplishment. Through God's leading to become an acupuncturist, I have been able to use this knowledge in treating others to this day. Like my mother taught me, first I go to the Lord in prayer and thanksgiving for his wisdom and insight. Then with my medical school training, I insert the needle as he directs.

In the meantime, I also graduated from the university with a bachelor's degree in music. My first job was teaching music at a middle school in Taipei, Taiwan. In addition, the Lord blessed me with many private piano students as well. Since I felt his leading for me to attend a graduate school in music overseas, I began saving all of my extra money for that purpose. It took me several years to accumulate enough for a master's degree program but through frugal planning, I saved my money carefully while I was applying for a graduate program in America.

While I was making my plans in 1974, my father decided he was ready to retire from his pharmacy job with the US Navy. He felt that it was time for a change in direction in his life. He and Mom were spending more of their free time practicing acupuncture and healing people. When he finally retired and had more free time available, Dad was invited to be a speaker at the gospel summer camp in New York City. Because he no longer worked full time in Taiwan, he decided to accept the offer to share his faith in America. With our church family's encouragement, my mother also accompanied him to the meetings. It turned out to be a pivotal decision for our family and shaped our future because they fell in love with America during their time of ministry at the camp.

It was a busy summer for our family. I was so excited and honored to have been accepted by the Florida State University (FSU) College of Music. It had a stellar reputation for an outstanding graduate program. The school awarded me with a graduate assistantship for my first year of study. That would certainly help with some of the financial burdens of school. God was clearly making his provision for me. Finally, I saved enough money for the two-year course of study and was ready to go. I was scheduled to move to America!

3

A Lesson in Tithing

The Lord Almighty speaks very clearly about tithing. In Malachi 3:10, he says, "Bring the whole tithe into the storehouse, that there may be food in my house. Test me in this… and see if I will not throw open the floodgates of heaven and pour out so much blessing that you will not have room enough for it."

I was packed and ready to go. Just days before I left Taiwan for my studies at FSU, the church I attended announced a serious need. There was no longer enough room in the current church building for the growing congregation as the church had outgrown its facilities. Determining that the old Japanese-style building must be torn down, the elders decided that an eight-story building should be built in its place to satisfy present and future growth. The difficulty was that there was not enough money for the project. The challenge was problematic. Although I was leaving for Florida to work on my master's degree, the Lord impressed upon me that I should give to this project for my church. It didn't make financial sense. I didn't have much money, certainly not any discretionary funds. My money was budgeted for the next two years. Saving the way I did, everything I had was designated for my studies overseas. Since I was leaving Taipei, this was not my problem. I wouldn't be attending church here anymore. All of these arguments raced through my mind, but it didn't matter. I clearly heard the Lord telling me to give. I did not hesitate. With a grateful and thankful heart, I offered one-tenth of the money that I had saved for my second year of graduate college. I was determined to be obedient. The church had been my "storehouse." I trusted God as he clearly challenged me to do in Malachi, so I gave with no regrets and much joy. Then I left for America.

How God proved himself to me! My obedience in tithing opened up blessing after blessing. Wonderful things ensued for me. During my first year at FSU, my mentor professor said that he wanted to recommend me for the university fellowship for my second year of study. I felt extremely honored by his regard but not very hopeful. The fellowship was exceptionally competitive. Only three students from the entire university would be awarded this prestigious award. I didn't have straight *A*s, didn't read or speak English well, and was from a foreign country. Clearly, there were far better candidates. But I serve a mighty God, and to my surprise and everlasting gratitude, I won! The value of the university fellowship awarded on my second year of study turned out to be *seventeen* times of the amount I gave to my church in Taiwan. The financial award was so great that I didn't even need to have a job to support myself during the second year of my master's program. What a blessing the Lord gave me! Such favor! It was not some simple coincidence that I received this, it was a direct and specific blessing from God. I tithed my savings for the second year of graduate school and the Lord abundantly multiplied the amount of the tithe and gave it back to me.

4

Mistakes and Blessings

During my first two years in America, I studied very hard at FSU and spent most of my free time practicing in the piano studio. From morning to evening, I worked at improving my piano performance. As important as practice was, I still hadn't forgotten my interest in acupuncture. At a talent show, I represented the Chinese international students by doing an acupuncture performance. A student from India who had problems with shoulders pains came on stage and asked me to try it on him. As I pulled the needles out of his body, he declared that he was totally healed. I praise God for equipping me with this skill. Through acupuncture, God healed many people with lower back problems, headaches, stomach pain, upper back pain, neck pain, and all types of muscular problems. Because God gave this gift to me, I did not charge for performing these treatments. I give him the glory and thanks.

I poured myself into my studies. After two years of intense practice and new learned techniques, I graduated with a master's degree in music education in 1976. Because of the university fellowship that the Lord provided for me, I was able to take extra classes and complete all of the required credits for a PhD. I didn't pursue my doctorate because I was recommended to a world-renowned piano professor, Agustin Anievas, who lived in New York. It was an unbelievable opportunity, an amazing blessing. I quickly agreed to study with him and decided to forgo the doctorate and obtain a second master's degree, this one in piano performance at Brooklyn College instead.

My parents' experience at the gospel camp convinced them to leave Taiwan and relocate to New York so my entire family immigrated to the United States at the same time. With God's guidance, Mom found the family a wonderful house in Flushing, New York. With four kids living together with our parents, it was a little crowded at times, but we did not get in each other's way because we were incredibly busy. My younger sisters were immersing themselves in English for school so they usually studied until midnight. James was studying extremely hard and soon was accepted into medical school. I was working on my piano performance. It was a matter of economics for all of us. Because of the money I saved from living with my family, I was able to afford my studies at Brooklyn College. While living in Flushing, an astonishing blessing occurred to me. My father purchased a Steinway & Sons grand piano for me. Such a dream come true! I now owned one of the best instruments ever made while I studied under one of the best piano teachers in the world! Both were incredible gifts from God. My teacher equipped me with new knowledge and skills and a higher level of musicianship during these two years of rigorous training while I practiced on a beautiful grand piano at home. The music which came from that piano was extraordinary.

Everything was going my way. I was finishing my second master's degree. I received many accolades for my music and achieved great success. These feelings of accomplishment and euphoria led me to focus more on myself and my capabilities, less on what God was doing for me through his blessing and provision. My desire for the will of the Lord waned. Pride in my own abilities escalated. I was on a rebellious path that would require tremendous personal payment for years to come. I finished my studies. Then with a willful and conceited heart, I married. In retrospect, I could honestly say that I heard the Lord tell me that this wasn't his best situation for me. But I was stubborn. I overheard my father talking about arranging a marriage for me, which really hurt my pride. I told myself that I could find my own husband. After all, I was an attractive and talented woman. Despite the fact that I had given the Lord jurisdiction in my decision making my entire life, I refused to listen to him about this. This time, I was going to do it my way. I didn't needed any help from either my earthly father or my heavenly Father. I was a strong, intelligent woman capable of making my own decisions, particularly with my personal life. I would be in control of this part of my life. I would choose my own husband and, if necessary, I would help him change. I knew best—or so I thought. The result was that I began my marriage by turning my back on God's voice. Letting pride dictate my decision making was extremely costly to me for years. It opened up the door to great pain in my life.

In 1978, we started our life together by leaving New York, all of my family, and everything that I knew and valued. My husband and I moved to Tallahassee, Florida, where he was a PhD student at the university. Since the Lord called me to teach piano rather than perform in concerts I found a teaching job but it was in Cordele, Georgia, hours away from our home. Boarding with an elderly lady during the work week, I drove home to Florida for the weekends in order to be with my husband. It was a difficult lifestyle. I tried very hard to make it work. It helped that I loved teaching and I loved my students. Teaching was my calling. I found great joy in the classroom. I poured my life into those children. Away from school, however, I was lonely. I didn't have a home church to attend so it was difficult to build a spiritual community. I was far from my husband and, for the majority of time, lived far away from our home. I was also far from the family I grew up with. I missed them so much. The best part of my week was when I talked to my family back in New York. Our telephone time gave me renewed strength until the next phone call. My sadness and loneliness must have seeped through our conversations because my father announced that he would make the trip to Florida in order to spend some time with me when school was out. I was so excited about this news. It would be wonderful to see him. I really needed to see my dad.

Dad came to Tallahassee to visit me in the summer of 1979. It exceeded my expectations. Not only did we vacation at Disney World and have a great time sightseeing, we enjoyed being with each other. I give thanks to God for the amazing time he gave me with my father! Every daughter wants to have her daddy's attention. Our time together was so perfect during that visit. It refreshed my soul and lifted my spirits. Although I did not know it then, it was our last time together. Later that fall after I had reported back to school, he called me and we had a wonderful conversation over the phone. He was so happy and joyful. He shared with me that he had gone with the church to upstate New York to pick apples. Rarely had I heard him so upbeat. It delighted my heart. I said goodbye to him with a smile on my lips. As I hung up the phone, I did not realize it would be the last time I would ever hear my father's voice. Two days later while I was teaching at Cordele, Georgia, I received terrible news. My dad was unconscious from a fall. He had been trying to fix the gutter on our family's house when he slipped off the roof. The fall had severely injured his head and he was in the hospital in a coma. I was horribly frustrated because I could not get off work to get to him and comfort him.

> *All people are like grass, and all their faithfulness is like the flowers of the field. The grass withers and the flowers fall, because the breath of the Lord blows on them. Surely the people are grass. The grass withers and the flowers fall, but the word of our God endures forever.* (Isa. 40:6–8)

Ten days later, he went home to be with the Lord. I was very thankful that we had time together during the summer. I remember him smiling at me and touching my hair. This memory still brings enormous comfort to me. I still miss my dad very much. Looking back at that special summer, I am so touched by God's faithfulness, that even while I had been in rebellion to him, he, nonetheless, cared for me and blessed me with this wonderful time. I received a great deal of solace from teaching my students and grew very close to them. They were so dear to me. Teaching for two years, I was carving my own little place in Georgia with my fellow teachers and friends. Joy was replacing my sorrow. The heaviness in my heart was slowly lifting. I was part of a community of caring and loving people. Happiness filled my heart as I recovered from grief. I began to laugh again.

Then my husband announced that we were going to move. He found a job where he could continue to work on his dissertation. I was heartbroken. With great reluctance, I said goodbye to all my students and colleagues. We moved to Poquoson, Virginia, close to Newport News and Hampton. I was so glad my mother came to help me in Virginia. I needed her. First, I lost my dad, then we moved and I felt uprooted from my job and my friends. Mom really made a difference during her visit. With her financial help, we moved into a beautiful, newly built house. I was so happy that we were being blessed with this house. I thank God that he put me there when my heart needed comforting. Chesapeake Bay was at the end of the road, an idyllic place. The peacefulness of the countryside comforted me. Poquoson was such a nice, quiet little town. My life developed a tranquil simplicity. I soon discovered a wonderful church that I attended by myself. My husband told me that he could not accompany me to church because he had to work on his dissertation.

The tranquility in our lives did not last for long! Brian, my first child, was born in May 1981. What a great gift from God he was! I loved being a mother. More importantly, I experienced contentment. The time in Virginia lasted five years, and it was a precious time with my little boy. While there were ongoing issues within my marriage, my life overall was very busy and fulfilling. I really did love teaching and taught many piano students. It was my calling. Little did I know that bigger changes were getting ready to shake me to the very core of my existence.

5

Struggling in Difficult Times

We moved again, which I did not want to do. Although not everything was perfect with my life in Virginia, I was very happy with my little boy and teaching. Once more, I built a life with which I was content. People in our community knew who I was, and I was well regarded and respected. I had purpose and success. With a move to a new community, I would have none of that.

When my husband's new job took us to Norman, Oklahoma, it was with a heavy heart I said goodbye to Virginia and all of my students. I felt uprooted and disoriented in my new life. I experienced great difficulty adjusting without a sense of community. Life grew bleaker after I gave birth to my second child, Hamilton. Although he was a sweet little boy, my life had grown into a living nightmare. I had two young children, one being a newborn, and had no outlet for myself. I knew nothing about how to be a good housewife. It was never-ending struggle day after day, week after week. I had never done this before. I had no help. I had no one to talk to. Now that we were in a new community, I didn't even have piano students to teach. Additionally, when he wasn't viciously demeaning me, my husband treated me as if I wasn't there. He ignored my pleas. I was isolated in a new town with no friends and no job. Because I had gotten into the habit of handling everything myself, I certainly didn't feel the presence of the Lord at all. I felt entirely alone. I was so isolated. I saw no one but my husband and kids. The emotional suffering was real and oppressive. It was hard to get up every morning to take care of my children. Hopelessness and helplessness crashed about me like waves on a rocky shore. I was drowning, sucked into an ocean of despair. My husband's crushing cruelty destroyed any esteem I had as a Chinese woman. Life was so dark for me, I felt hopeless. There was no help to be found. There was nowhere to turn.

Of course, I was wrong. Sadly, I had grown complacent about my relationship with the Lord so I wasn't looking to him for answers. I was still trying to handle things myself with my own power and in my own way. Looking back, I know now that I should have immediately turned to the Almighty God for help, but I was ignoring the Lord's outstretched arms wanting to rescue me. It was a vicious circle. I kept trying to solve things by myself and I kept failing. Then I would try to solve things myself and again I would fail. Each failure brought me to a lower level of depression in my life. I was in a free fall of pain just waiting to crash and fragment into a thousand pieces. Desperation dictated my actions. I knew that I could not keep living like this or I would die.

Things got so bad that in the summer of 1989, I had to flee to save my life. My mother needed help caring for other grandchildren. To escape the nightmare that had become my life, I left for New York City to help her out. Mom made room for me and my two sons. I never believed in running away, but that was exactly what I was doing. Running away from problems never solves anything, and running away from God leads to deeper morass of unhappiness. I lived with my mother in New York for six months. Nothing worked out the way I envisioned. My mom was caring for Victor who was two and Bernadette, a newborn. With my own two boys, it felt like the walls were closing in on top of us. Then on top of everything else, I developed health issues and had to have surgery. I didn't think things could get worse but they certainly did.

The day after I returned from the hospital, little Bernadette died suddenly in her sleep, a crib death. The whole family was in chaos, hurting and in mourning. It was clear to me that I could not stay in New York anymore. Under the circumstances, I decided that

I needed to take my two children back to Oklahoma to live with my husband. My older child, Brian, encouraged me to go home and take his father to church so that he could learn about God, but nothing had been resolved with him during this time. I felt absolutely hopeless. I saw no way out. Anguish and despondency flooded over me as I faced the reality of returning home to more days of darkness in my soul. During this difficult time in my life, a significant hindrance was that I kept looking to myself to solve my problems and figure out the answers. I had no solutions; I had no answers. I was sinking deeper and deeper into despair. Rather than relying on my own strength, I should have been going to my heavenly Father to guide me and deliver me out of my pain. That's how I was raised, that's what I knew to do, but I had gotten way off track in my spiritual life.

As I mentioned earlier, I was born in a Christian family, raised in church, baptized at the age of twelve, and attended Sunday school and Sunday worship every week. My mother taught the six of us children how to pray and memorize Bible verses. Every Sunday night, there was a time for the Lord's Supper, praise, and prayers in my home. I attended a lot of church activities. All of this gave me a great foundation for my Christian faith but I was still spiritually immature. Sometimes my important decision making was based only upon my common sense and, of course, my own will. Too often it was about what I wanted and I needed. When I had the time, I would open the Bible and usually read wherever it happened to open. Of course I honored God, but I had not always given him all precedence in all things at all times. One problem was that the piano grew to be my first priority. When I was a child, it was not that obvious because my parents would help guide me. As I grew older, this lack of serious commitment created situations where I suffered many serious consequences due to my decisions.

6

Repentance and Return to God

If we confess our sins, he is faithful and just and will forgive us our sins and purify us from all unrighteousness.
—1 John 1:9

Once back at home in Norman, things only got worse for me. At our first dinner back, my husband announced that I had to repay every dime he ever spent on me to support me since the beginning of our marriage. Although my money had always been his money, I did not argue. I had nowhere else to go and nothing else that I could do. I was at the end of my rope. I admitted to myself that I was miserable being my own boss. Finally, I gave up my pride and turned to the Lord. It was either that or truly die. On bended knee with a repentant heart, I came to God, asking for a miracle. I had no other place to turn. My ways and my decisions led me down a road of death. I had tangled myself into a situation so dire that I required the kind of help that only the Almighty God could give. Choosing him meant choosing life, a new life and a new way of doing things. I chose God. He turned my life around with hope, vision, and purpose.

There was no ordained pastor in the church I attended with my boys. We had a substitute pastor, a student from Singapore. She attended Oklahoma Baptist University (OBU). This substitute pastor felt that our church needed a new class called Experiencing God, based upon the book written by Henry Blackaby. The purpose of the study was to grow closer to God in a more mature and disciplined manner. Well, that certainly pertained to my needs! I had been so busy trying to be in control of my life that I gave no time for God's leadership. Then I was busy reacting to the consequences of my poor decisions. My life was a chaotic, hurtful mess. It was time to pass the reign of my life over to him. I knew God and had experienced his great love and great blessings, but I hadn't matured in a disciplined way. Almost everything I knew had been spoon-fed to me by my mother. I resolved at this point in my life, much like the prodigal son, that only the Father could help me.

I bought the book and signed up for the course. At the very back of the book, I had to sign a form that I agreed to the requirements of the course. I added a prayer at the bottom of the page, "God, please wake me up at 6:00 a.m." I had become so depressed that I could not get up in the morning at all. As I started my life anew, it was clear that I needed God's help in every area of my life. This class was three months long. From the very first day of this commitment, my eyes flew open exactly at six in the morning. God heard and answered my simple prayer. He helped me to wake up early every morning. With that extra time, I began to pray, read my Bible assignments, memorize verses, and answer the study questions of the day. The discipline of the class gave me the structure to grow in God's grace.

Slowly, I changed. Where once my life and my soul had been in a total blackness of turmoil, I began to glimpse moments of joy and peace that grew daily. The more I studied, the more the Lord filled me with a lightness. He helped me go through the entire class while I built a personal, direct, individual, and intimate love relationship with Jesus. I learned that I was precious and honored in God's sight. He rebuilt my destroyed self-esteem. My life changed. Although I was still in the same miserable environment, I was no longer unhappy. I was no longer ashamed of my mistakes and disobedience. Because I was forgiven and a new person in Christ, I grew into a different person, a happy person. Sovereign God sustained and strengthened me, and my life was filled with his love and joy. Returning to his protective love, I was led to repent for the sin of taking charge of my life rather than allowing him to lead and guide me. As I did, peace flooded through me as his forgiveness washed over me. Since that day so many years ago, I continued to rise early, starting each morning with prayer and study of his word. Every year I go through the Bible in its entirety. At first, I spent a lot of time translating Chinese into English and then studying the English dictionary as I learned new vocabulary. With the Holy Spirit as my teacher, I overcame difficult passages and it became easier for me to study. Praise God! There was a dramatic change in my life.

One Sunday morning, the father of my children decided to attend church with us. In the middle of worship, he leaned over and told me that he was laid off from his job. He did not need to go to work on Monday. I was shocked and did not know how to respond. I prayed to God that I would be able to continue to make a tithe because without my household money, I wouldn't be able to make the offering to my church. During my daily devotional time for the next morning, I read in Exodus 22:29, "Do not hold back offerings from your granaries or your vats." That was my answer. I obeyed God's word and kept giving my monthly offering to my church in faith and the Lord continued to bless me by giving me back more in return.

Early in the year 2001, I planned a trip for my family. I wanted the four of us to go to Disney World in Florida. I thought it would be a nice time for my sons and their father to enjoy one another. It would be the first trip together for my husband and me since we were married. It was very expensive and took all my money that I saved over the years. I thought it would be a wonderful memory for my children. As I was planning the trip, I was told that I would receive four extra airplane tickets if I was willing to change my schedule to another day. I quickly agreed. Four free airline tickets! Now we could afford to attend Brian's graduation in Ithaca, New York, the next year. I praised God for responding to my obedience regarding finances. When we arrived at Disney World, our rental car had to be upgraded because all of the ones in the category we booked were all rented. They gave us a van to travel in. It was so roomy and comfortable. Again, I praised God for his faithfulness.

My family loved to eat seafood, especially lobster. In Oklahoma, it was very expensive so we didn't get to eat it very much. While driving through Florida, we saw a huge lobster sign above a seafood restaurant. It was advertising an early bird special for all-you-can-eat lobster from 4:00 to 6:00 p.m. Such a feast! The four of us enjoyed our wonderful dinner. Another blessing from the Lord! After the wonderful time we had in Florida, I began praying to the Lord that the father of my children find a job. This would be difficult because he really wasn't looking. He was still expecting me to give him money every week. I prayed, "Heavenly Father, I give thanks to you for your provision for me. Please help me pay him back with a positive attitude even though this request is so unreasonable." In less than two weeks, a job in Washington DC opened for him. At first he did not want to do it, but the company said that they would train him for the job and pay him very well. Reluctantly, he took the job. He left at the end of April 2002. I must say that I gave thanks to God. By refinancing the house in Oklahoma, God provided us a good house in Burke, Virginia, with a great school district. My youngest son Hamilton wanted to attend the school there and live in this house that God provided. Soon, Hamilton and his father made the move.

I was now alone in the house in Norman, Oklahoma. It was difficult to get deep sleep and wake up rested since I was not used to living alone. One dark night, I heard footsteps coming from the stairway. I was so frightened. Trembling in my bed, I sat up and listened. The steps thundered once more. I finally told myself that if someone kills me tonight, I will then be in heaven with Jesus. There is nothing better than that! Comforted, I relaxed in that knowledge. The Lord was in control of my life or my death. I waited, secure in the outcome of the evening. The noises continued. *Thump, thump, thump.* No one came to my room. Still, I was at complete peace in God's love and security. *Thump, thump, thump.* I wondered, *Why were they just walking up and down my stairs?* Then it occurred to me. The noises were not from my staircase, but my attic! It must be a raccoon who had gotten itself trapped in the attic. I laughed out loud and thanked God. He had taught me how to face death. I was no longer afraid to stay alone at home all night. The Lord will never forsake me. I have nothing to be afraid of.

The next day, I found several vents of the house had been torn open so I had them fixed. When a bad smell enveloped the house, I discovered a dead raccoon above the garage. As I had it removed, I continued to praise God that he set me free from fear. The Lord continued to move in my life as I surrendered my life back to him. During the years since I had left Virginia, I had no piano students and no way of earning a living. My passion for teaching had gone unfulfilled in Oklahoma. But God is an awesome provider. As I grew closer to him, he gave me back my career. It started with just a few piano students. One of these students was the wife of a famous University of Oklahoma (OU) basketball coach. She brought a television crew from the local NBC affiliate, KFOR, to film her piano lesson with me. There I was during the evening broadcast, teaching in front of the entire state of Oklahoma. Never could I have afforded that kind of marketing. Then a famous brain surgeon came to study with me. After he completed his neurosurgical procedures in the operating room, he would go practice on the Steinway piano on display at his hospital. Playing helped him to calm down after complicated surgeries. His piano performances drew large audiences at the hospital. It was free advertisement. The Lord brought me additional students, such as the children of hospital staff, nurses, and aides as well as physicians and their families. I was so blessed.

My business continued to grow. At a local piano competition, all three of the winners were my students and I was featured along with them in the newspaper. One of my gifted students was the first place winner at the Oklahoma City Philharmonic piano concerto competition. It seemed that my students and I were in the media constantly. The Lord just enveloped this work with favor and blessing. I continued to give thanks for the achievements he bestowed upon my students and myself. It was nothing short of miraculous. The following year was even more exceptional. I had really good piano students and their parents were extremely supportive. More and more of my students won the competitions they entered. My fame as a piano teacher grew. My practice grew to such an extent that the Lord had to provide me a larger piano studio from which to teach. I prospered spiritually and financially.

> *Now to him who is able to do immeasurably more than all we ask or imagine, according to his power that is at work within us, to him be glory in the church and in Christ Jesus throughout all generations, for ever and ever! Amen.* (Eph. 3:20–21)

7

Through a Mother's Prayer

The Lord God continued to bless me in so many ways. In the summer of 2009, my younger son Hamilton graduated from college. Like many college graduates, he was looking for a job. Staying with my mother in New York City, he sent out his resume over and over. I prayed for him daily. At times, it seemed like my prayers were going nowhere. Even I felt the futility of his situation, but I was his mother and I was not going to quit. I continued to pray for him. One day in December while I was in prayer over my son and his job search, I heard the Holy Spirit say, "I have heard your prayers. Now, it's time to praise and give thanks to the Lord while you pray over your son."

My heart thrilled at God's words. However, nothing seemed to happen at first. I saw nothing different, no immediate changes. Hamilton kept looking for a job. But in my prayers, I praised the Lord for Hamilton's job. Just as he instructed, I thanked the Lord for the wonderful job he would provide for my son. In February, Hamilton called. He had an interview with GEICO in Washington DC. He was so nervous that he did not have a good night's sleep the previous night. His interview had gone very badly, his answers were all wrong. He was extremely upset and discouraged from the experience. He waited for months to get a job interview only to have it blow up in his face. He was driving from Washington back home to New York when he called me to tell me all about it. As he related the horrible experience to me, I told him not to worry about it. I knew that God was in control, because I had committed Hamilton's job hunt to God. I said, "You must learn your lesson from this failure so you will respond better next time. I know that you have a job. The Lord has told me so." An hour later, Hamilton called me again. He was so excited, he shouted, "Mom, I got the job! The company just called. I start work in two weeks."

Praise God! Hamilton knew deeply in his heart that this job offer was from the Lord God Almighty. He didn't even make it back to New York. My sister Gladis lived in New Jersey. Hamilton drove up to her house, borrowed some clothes from his cousins, ate dinner with them, and headed back to Virginia to get ready to start work. I thank God for answering my prayers and teaching us this very important lesson in trusting in him.

8

Understanding through Scripture

Instead of using my Chinese Bible, I now studied from an English version and read through the entire Bible each year. But there was still a verse I just didn't understand.

- Hebrews 1:14 says, "Are not all angels ministering spirits sent to serve those who will inherit salvation?"

What did that mean? It was my morning devotional memory verse but I was no closer to understanding it than the last time I read it. Nonetheless, I memorized it and got on with my day.

I started on my morning errands with the first stop at the bank to deposit money for my offering. As I left the bank, I looked carefully in both directions as usual. The way was clear. I turned left. All of a sudden, a yellow car appeared in front of me. We were going to collide! I cried out to God, "Protect me!" Miraculously, the accident did not happen. There was a protection in front of my car. Immediately, I heard the Holy Spirit telling me, "Now do you understand your memory verse that you studied this morning?" Yes, Lord. I do now! Praise God for saving my life.

One day, I received an urgent phone call from my church. A woman possessed by an evil spirit needed help. The church was to hold a prayer meeting that night and believers were invited to go and pray for her. This was not something that I particularly wanted to be a part of, but I went to the Lord in prayer, asking him to lead me in this situation. He told me that I was to go and pray for this troubled soul. I felt nervous to be around her. I had never been around this situation before and really didn't want to go so I questioned the Lord again. "I'm afraid to be around this. What shall I do?" God answered, "Go. I will be with you."

As we gathered together that evening, I kept my distance from her while Pastor Lam prayed and read Bible verses to her. As time passed the woman mutilated herself by scratching and gouging herself with her long jagged fingernails. She was really hurting herself. The pastor's wife asked if anyone had some fingernail clippers so that she could trim the woman's nails. I had some clippers in my purse, which I kept for my sons. As I reached for them, I heard God tell me to cut her fingernails for her. I quickly asked him to hold her hands still so I wouldn't hurt her. Her eyes were squeezed shut as I approached her. While I was cutting her fingernails, I told her to let her heart cry out to Jesus to save her from this oppression. Her hands stilled, she quieted. I was so thankful that I could finish without causing her any harm.

Several months later while I was shopping for groceries at a supermarket, a lady behind me called out to me and thanked me for helping her. I turned around and to my surprise, it was the woman from the prayer vigil. I asked her, "How did you know it was me? Your eyes were tightly closed when I trimmed your nails for you. You never saw me." She answered, "I recognized your voice because you kept saying, 'Let your heart cry out to Jesus to save you!'" She revealed to me that an entire legion of demons had overtaken her because she used to practice sorcery back in her hometown. They tormented and oppressed her because she opened the door to them through her use of witchcraft.

The Lord is so awesome. He allowed me to know what had happened to her. Praise God! She was free of the darkness that possessed her. I was so grateful that our paths had crossed. Where I had originally felt trepidation about ministering to her, the Lord replaced that fear with a great compassion for her because I knew that the Lord in me was stronger than any demon. 1 John 4:4 says, "You, dear children, are from God and have overcome them, because the one who is in you is greater than the one who is in the world."

9

While Traveling in China

As I mentioned earlier, both of my parents fled their hometown in China and immigrated to Taiwan in 1949 to avoid political persecution. For twenty-four years, there was absolutely no contact with any family members behind the Bamboo Curtain. It was forbidden by the Chinese government. It could lead to imprisonment and death. When they arrived in America in 1974, my parents received their green cards quickly because my father was a pharmacist. Two years later, my mother received the sad news that my grandmother died. My mother grieved. She never had a chance to say goodbye and now she never would. Her heart overflowed with sorrow not only from the loss of her mother, but for all the family she left behind. Because she and my dad, along with her older brother, left China so quickly, she never had the opportunity to let any of her family members know she was leaving.

Over the years, the situation in China slowly eased. Communication and travel became possible. Finally in 1986, Mom had the opportunity to return to her homeland for a visit. She was so excited. Because my father passed away seven years earlier, my brother James traveled with her as she visited all of her family as well as the relatives of my father. She was there for eight weeks. That trip meant so much to her. However, when she returned to America, her brother Ze Rong, sent her a letter from China, wanting to end their relationship. She showed me the letter. It was extremely unkind. I empathized with her confusion and pain. She did not understand why he would send her such a letter. While visiting her homeland, Mom discovered that her parents' ashes were kept in a tower in Tin Jing where her younger sister used to live. That bothered her. After she returned home, she had a fervent wish. She wanted to go back to China to bury her parents' ashes in the Chinese village of Zhai, my grandmother's birthplace. It was also her hope to resolve the issue with her brother as well. In 2005, she contacted her relatives and made all of the necessary arrangements for travel but had to cancel because of health problems. I told her that I would go in her place.

> *Hezekiah received the letter from the messenger and read it. Then he went to the temple of the Lord and spread it out before the Lord. And Hezekiah prayed to the Lord…so that all the kingdoms of the earth may know that you alone, Lord, are God.* (2 Kings. 19:14–15, 19)

Like Hezekiah, I wrote down my needs and expectations. I went to the Lord with my list for the upcoming trip and began daily praying over it. I wrote:

- bury my grandparents,
- share the gospel with my Chinese relatives,
- discover what happened with my mother's younger brother, Ze Rong,
- explore my heritage by visiting my parents' hometowns,
- get some medications I needed,
- have my teeth fixed (since the prices are so much lower there),
- visit my mother's hometown church,
- do tourist stuff like visiting the Great Wall, Summer Palace, the Altar of Heaven in Beijing, and sightseeing in Qingdao and Shandong,
- and purchase a couple of designer handbags.

In August, it was finally time to leave for China. I had been in prayer for eight months regarding this trip. As excited as I was about visiting my ancestors' homeland, I was more excited about what God was going to do on this trip. I had great expectations. I caught the plane in Oklahoma City and flew to Chicago. From Chicago, I had a nonstop flight to Beijing. This trip was a gift for my mother. It was also a way for me to serve my Lord. I wanted to serve him in every way for every single day of this great journey.

The adventure began immediately. Like all travelers, I was curious about who would share this long trip in the seats next to me on the airplane. A Chinese couple from Canada visiting China sat beside me. After we all were seated and began talking, I finally asked them, "Have you ever heard about Jesus?" Their eyes lit up! "Of course!" they said. "We are believers." We were immediately fast friends. We had a delightful time talking about our Christian experiences. We traded stories of how we came to the Lord and experienced salvation. My new friends told me that before they were believers, they were invited to a God-filled church. After visiting for a while, they began to attend a Bible study as well. It was at the Bible study where their hearts began to soften. They began to see the truth of the scripture. Eventually, they stepped out in faith and accepted Jesus in their hearts.

During the conversation, they mentioned that there was a tragedy that happened in Toronto. A desperate man drove himself up to a mountain highway and jumped off, killing himself. As a young man, he was regarded as an outstanding athlete, receiving the prestigious first place win in martial arts in China. Not only did he excel in the Chinese martial arts, he was also an exceptional Chinese scholar and graduated from the prestigious Tsinghua University in China. He received his PhD in America in nuclear physics. Despite his qualifications, however, he, could not find a job anywhere. He thought that more training might help so he decided to pursue an additional degree. He traveled to Canada and received his second doctorate in chemistry. He still couldn't find a job. Even though he was a great athlete and scholar, it wasn't enough. Even though he was married with two small children, it wasn't enough. Even though he was dedicated and a hard worker, it wasn't enough. Because he did not see that his value was based upon how Jesus saw him, nothing would ever be enough to fill his deep need for affirmation. Only in Jesus can one find that kind of validation. The Chinese couple sitting next to me continued describing how the Chinese community in Canada was trying to raise money for his survivors. It was heartbreaking on so many levels.

This story was still on my mind as I arrived in Shandong and met my Chinese relatives for the first time. Fan Ming, the oldest brother on my father's side, hosted my visit. Seven of my cousins gathered to greet me. They were excited. I was their American relative, the first one they had ever met. Ranging in age from eight to seventeen, my cousins were eager to try out their English on me as they welcomed me to their home and country. Each one of them mentioned how they wanted to come to America and pursue their PhD degrees. While I was trying to keep their names straight in the midst of all their chattering, the Holy Spirit prompted me to share the sad story of the brilliant young man who had just ended his life several days ago in Canada.

I asked them, "What is the purpose of your life?" Again they explained to me their desire to attend a university in America and earn PhDs. "While a worthy goal, it is not the true purpose of the life you live." I then shared with my extended family the terrible story I heard on my trip over here on the airplane. "If only someone had shared with him about who Jesus is." At their quizzical looks, I continued, "Jesus is the Son of God incarnate, born of the Virgin Mary. He came to the world as a man, lived a sinless life, and died on the cross, thereby paying the penalty of our sins and satisfying God's wrath toward sinful men. He redeemed and reconciled the relationship between God and men. Jesus was resurrected from the dead. He is alive and is right now sitting at the right hand of God. He is the creator of the whole universe; everything was created through him, for him, and by him. Nothing is too difficult for him. Nothing! Believe in Jesus and confess your sin and repent. Then you too can become a child of God. Now think about that man who killed himself in Canada. He had so much going for him but he did not have a job and, more importantly, he did not believe in Jesus. Would it have been too hard for God to give that young man a job? Of course not. But how sad is it that a man who had earned two prestigious doctorates, was an accomplished athlete, and loved by a beautiful family could not personally handle the difficult situation of not finding a job. His sense of purpose came from what he could accomplish, and it was not enough. Only Jesus is enough. Rather than choosing hope and life through Jesus, he sought death. Instead of walking in contentment and joy by committing to Jesus, discouragement and a lack of self-esteem drove him to end his life. His death was not necessary. It was a waste!" I asked each of them, "Why are you wasting time? Today is your day to make this decision. Who among you are ready to accept Jesus as your Savior? Who believes that he is the Son of God? God was powerful enough to raise Jesus from the dead. He will help you through your difficulties and challenges as well." Each person of the Chinese family I just met raised a hand. Every one of them asked Jesus into their heart and became Christians. All were saved that day. Praise God for his mercy and glory! This was a work of the Lord, not mine. I was just the mouthpiece. The Lord God saved them all. Such a glorious day!

The next day, I was escorted by some of my cousins to the village of Zhai where many of my mother's family lived. As I was getting to know these new family members, my relatives shared that my uncle Ze Rong, the younger brother of my mother, was coming to Zhai from his home in Qingdao. He was bringing my grandmother's ashes for a burial ceremony and was even going to erect a tombstone. I was in shock. That's exactly what I planned to do. Without any communication between the two of us, we both had the same idea at the same point in time. It was a miracle! God led me to China at the most perfect time. I explained to my family my purpose for being there and that I was doing it on behalf of my mother. The family was awestruck. One of my cousins said, "Your God is the true God!" I certainly agreed. God sent me across the world to be in China at the perfect time. I was also thankful that my uncle would arrive in three days so we could discuss the "end of relationship" letter he sent to my mother. I needed to know the facts. It was time to resolve all questions and heal the pain. God put everything together so that I could accomplish what I had planned to do in order to satisfy my mother's wish. The Lord is truly omnipotent. There was only one task left for me to do. I promised Mom I would honor her with beautiful flowers at the ceremony so I needed to have them delivered.

With everything underway in Zhai, I traveled to my father's hometown of Bo Shan, a beautiful mountainous region. The city was surrounded by many small hills and mountain ranges. Cousin Yi Lai took me to climb the mountains. It was glorious and absolutely beautiful during our ascent. My senses were overwhelmed by God's creation—the sweet air, the clear sky, and the majestic mountains. Such a perfect day! In the middle of the hike, I saw a spring on the side of the trail. The sign read, "Living Water." It provided hikers with free drinking water to counteract dehydration from the thin air. After drinking, we felt revived and refreshed. Immediately, the Holy Spirit impressed upon me to explain to my cousin the true meaning of *living water*. I began talking about how Jesus Christ is the true living water, providing life and vitality for all believers unto eternity. Without the real living water, there is no hope or meaning in our lives. There is only death. Yi Lai looked at me and said that when he was a young boy, he attended Sunday school. He heard about Jesus there but had never accepted him into his heart to be his Savior. Yi Lai told me that he very much wanted to do so now. At that very moment on the side of a mountain in China, my cousin accepted Jesus. Praise the Lord! He was saved that day.

After we went back to his home, I met yet another cousin, Li Hua. The two of us bonded immediately. As a physician, she took me shopping for my medical list. With her help, I quickly purchased all the medicine I needed without any problems. What a blessing! We had enough time left over to tour the city of Bo Shan. It was a lovely interlude. She invited me to stay with her while I remained in China and treated me like a beloved sister. We even looked alike! My own two younger sisters, Gladis and Gloria, who met her two years earlier, told me the very same thing. Li Hua and I spent many hours together while I visited China. Our time was joyous and kept me from missing my home and my family. Her hospitality was extremely generous. She provided a feast of dumplings in my honor, and we had wonderful fellowship.

On Sunday morning, I went to church with an aunt from my father's side. We arrived right on time. To my surprise, the church was already packed. There were no empty seats at all. From one end of the church to the other in every pew, all were praying with bowed heads. Hundreds of black-haired heads were bowed down before our Lord Jesus. It was an unforgettable scene. Some people made room for us so we could squeeze in. Upon being seated, I immediately bowed my own head. The Lord began speaking to me. I heard his voice saying, "Do you love me?" I replied, "Yes, of course I love you." A second time, Jesus asked me the same question, "Lily, do you love me?" I answered, "Yes, Lord. You know that I love you. It's the reason why I came here. I want my kinsfolk to know you and to study your word." A third time, Jesus asked me the same question, "Do you love me?" Comprehension dawned in my heart. I understood what I was being asked. I realized that no, I didn't love him like these reverent people around me. They were always in danger for celebrating their faith. They lived every moment and were prepared to give up their lives because of their love for Jesus. I did not. My Christianity was convenient and easy. Although I might think that I had grown into a woman of great faith, compared to these Chinese Christian brothers and sisters, I was only lukewarm. These people understood true sacrifice. They lived in constant peril because of their faith. I realized that they revered our God much more than I did. I resolved then and there to dedicate myself to a deeper walk with Jesus—a more serious walk, a more intense walk. Although, I had witnessed for Him here in China and at home, I could do more and I wanted to do more. I wanted to live for God in such a wholehearted way that people would always see the heavenly Father whenever they saw me or whenever I spoke. With a bowed head in a Chinese church halfway across the world, I committed myself to a more intense fellowship with Christ.

The day came for the burial ceremony at my grandmother's grave. It was important to my mother that I take flowers on her behalf and lay them on the grave. I searched all over town but could not find flowers anywhere! I was so disappointed with myself. How could I represent my mother without any flowers? She had specifically asked me to do this. With a hurting heart, I asked the Lord to please help me with this impossible problem. After fifteen minutes, my uncle Ze Rong, my mother's estranged youngest brother, arrived from Qingdao with his family with two bouquets of flowers. When he heard of my dilemma, he graciously said, "One is for you, Lily. I brought them from Qingdao out of respect for your mother." Praise God for his mercy and faithfulness. I quickly thanked him for answering my prayer. I also thanked my uncle for this great kindness to my mother. My heart warmed toward him. This was not the man I was expecting to meet. Rather than being aloof and hostile, he was considerate and loving. I liked him right away.

As a family, we went to the gravesite. All was ready. I prayed for the ceremony to bring honor to the Lord. We took lots of photos so that I could show them to my mother. I was so happy that my grandparents' ashes had been returned and buried in my mom's home village, the birthplace of my grandmother. God granted a desire of my mother's heart. Later, my cousins prepared a big feast of at least twenty courses, including fried green onion pita bread, dumplings, and noodles. This level of hospitality touched my heart. I was overwhelmed by this level of affection and acceptance. During dinner, I asked Uncle Ze Rong if I could go to Qingdao with his family. He answered yes immediately. He added that he would buy the bus ticket for me. I couldn't believe his great kindness toward me. There was absolutely no evidence of any hard feelings. When I arrived at Qingdao, I was greeted by my uncle and his wife. They made me feel at home. I really felt loved and welcomed by them. I brought up the separation letter that he had written to my mother that broke her heart.

"I did not write such a letter," he protested. "I thought she did not write me because she did not want a relationship with me since I was poor!" I considered what he was telling me. He didn't write because she hadn't written and she didn't write because she thought he didn't want a relationship with her. What a dreadful misunderstanding! My uncle told me that he needed to write a letter right now to my mom. "I want you to take it to her," he said. The moment he started writing, I could tell that he told me the truth. He had not written the separation letter. The Chinese characters of his penmanship were totally different than those in the letter Mom had received. Praise God! The Lord had gently cleared up this misunderstanding. Although they were never able to determine who did write the cruel letter, it did not matter. The relationship between my mother and uncle was restored.

I had several things left to do. Before I came to China, I heard that dental treatment was much cheaper in China than it was in the USA. I badly needed my teeth worked on so dental work was high on the list which I prayed over before I left. I had not yet found the other item on my list, a new handbag, but had heard that there were supposed to be some places nearby to find bargains. I brought both of these items to my aunt's attention and asked if she had any recommendations for me. She did not know of any places that sold designer purses but she knew a dentist who recently retired. She had a great reputation and lived just around the corner. Since she was willing to see me, my aunt took me to her immediately. She made molds for the two front teeth as well as another tooth in the back of my mouth. She told me it would only take a couple of days to make the crowns. I could have my teeth taken care of before I flew home. It was another miracle!

While I stayed in Qingdao with my aunt and uncle, my cousin Yi-Qing took me sightseeing and showed me the countryside. Qingdao is a city on the sea. I found it beautiful. Mom had told me many stories about Qingdao. Nothing had been exaggerated. It was simply amazing! I decided to swim in the sea although I was not good at swimming. I had so much fun. After we swam, Yi-Qing took me to other famous tourist spots. One of the first places he took me was the Taoist temple at Mount Lau. Before we could pass through the gate, the lady tour guide explained the rules to us and emphasized the importance of following them. I witnessed about Jesus to her and then warned her against worshipping idols like those found in the temple. We walked through the entrance and climbed up the slope of the mountain.

Yi-Qing and I talked about my grandmother and her relationship with the Lord. I found out that he had taken care of my grandmother during the later stages of her life. A good man, he went to help her every single day because she was paralyzed and could not leave her bed. He was confused, however, because every morning when he arrived to help, our grandmother was out of bed and on her knees leaning over it. He couldn't understand how she was able to get out of her bed without help, let alone what she was doing on her knees. I told him, "Grandmom was praying to God for you!" At his look of shock, I added, "And God has sent me to you to share about his great love for you." I explained the plan of salvation to him, that Jesus is the Son of God. He came to earth, was born of the Virgin Mary, died on the cross, and paid the penalty for our sin. He defeated death and was resurrected from the dead after three days in the tomb. Jesus is the sacrificial atonement. His shed blood wipes away our sins, and whoever believes in him will not perish but have eternal life. Then and there, out in the open in front of anyone who might walk by, my cousin Yi-Qing accepted Christ. When he opened his eyes after the salvation prayer, he looked toward the heavens and said to me, "I have never noticed that the sky is so blue and beautiful." Praise be to my God! He heard and answered my grandmother's prayer for her grandson, Yi-Qing. I was so happy and honored to be his instrument in all of this.

While I stayed in Qingdao, I met yet another cousin. Joy was a lovely Christian woman. Her father was my uncle who had fled to Taiwan with my parents all those years ago. Three years older than me, she was little more than a baby when he had to leave his family behind to escape China. She had never seen her father again after that. It was so wonderful meeting her and getting acquainted. She loves the Lord very much and bravely serves at a local church. Although separated by continents and oceans, our God eventually restored the relationship between her and her father. I know why Joy had her name and was glad to meet this precious cousin.

During my last week in this beautiful city, I returned to the dentist. My teeth were fixed, which only cost three hundred dollars! The Lord blessed me with yet another miracle! I was very pleased with the end results and it felt great having my dental work all done. I still wanted to see more sights in my parents' homeland so I asked cousin Yi-Qing if it was possible to take a trip to Beijing. He told me that it would be no problem. He worked for the railroad and made all the arrangements for me and bought me the very best train ticket so I could sleep during the train ride.

With three bunks on each side of the sleeper car, there were several of us sharing the same first class train compartment. A boy across the car caught my eye. He was about eleven years old and traveling by himself. He packed some junk food and was eating nonstop. When he looked over at me, I asked him, "Have you ever heard about the Lord God?" His answer was that he was really smart and had a lot of knowledge about science and history. He also declared that he knew a lot about God as well. Despite his claim, I went ahead and clearly explained salvation to him saying, "John 3:16 states that God loves you so much that he gave his only Son Jesus to die for all of us. Whoever believes in him will not perish but will have eternal life." The boy sat quietly, thinking over my words.

From the top bunk, a twelve-year-old girl climbed down to talk to me. Her name was Yi-Wen. She asked me, "Who is this God you were talking about? Is he one of the gods in Greek mythology or is he the God of Noah's ark?" I told her that the God Almighty is the God of Noah's ark. I said, "He is the Creator of the entire universe. Nothing is impossible for him. I believe that he sent me today to be on the same train as you so that I could meet you and tell you about the wonderful Lord Jesus." Very openly, she started sharing her problems with me. Her father was a pilot. She missed her daddy a lot as they didn't get to see each other very often. The purpose of her trip to Qingdao was to spend time with him there. She was also extremely worried about her grandfather's health. He wasn't doing very well and had been ill. Between yearning for her father and worrying about her grandfather, she was in tears. "Can God help me?" Yi-Wen sobbed out loud to me. I told her that if she repented of her sins, accepted Jesus into her heart as her Lord and Savior, and prayed in Jesus' name, God would hear and answer her prayers. Immediately, she accepted Jesus as her Savior. At the end of her prayer, she said in English, "Thank you, Jesus!"

Yi-Wen's mother then came down from her upper bunk. She was a chemistry professor at Beijing University. She totally agreed with Christianity and said that China really needed Jesus and that the Chinese people could only be helped by God Almighty! I suggested that she find a Bible-believing church in Beijing and take Yi-Wen to worship there. Now that the little girl knew Jesus, she needed to be around other believers.

When the train arrived in Beijing, my cousin Yi-Qing took me to his cousin's home in the city. I was warmly welcomed by them. The next day, Yi-Qing and his cousin took me touring all of the historical sights. I only had two days to see everything, I could hardly wait to get started. The first place we visited was the Great Wall of China. Pictures do not do it justice. It was enormous! I was so excited to try to climb it! I climbed the Great Wall from the bottom all the way to the top! Such an experience! My cousin could not believe that I had made it in my first attempt. "How could you accomplish this?" asked Yi-Qing. I laughed and gave thanks to God for helping me because I didn't know that I could do it either!

From the Great Wall, we went to the Summer Palace. My history lessons from school came alive as we visited the old king's palace, the Temple of Heaven, and Tiananmen Square. We also tried a variety of amazing foods. I ate roasted Beijing duck and had hot pot at the foot of the temple. It was some of the most delicious food I've ever eaten in my life. Although it was summertime, the restaurant had air-conditioning so we ate in relative comfort. What a great adventure, one of the best in my life!

Sitting in the airplane during my return home, I reflected upon my travels since I left Oklahoma. I prayed and thanked God. My heart was overflowing with praise and thankfulness. Except for the fact that I never found a designer handbag while in China, the Lord had granted me all that I had asked of him. I told the Lord that it was all right that I didn't get new designer bags. I was just so appreciative for all that he had done in my life. My grateful heart spent the entire trip, praising him as I made the long journey from Beijing back to New York City.

10

Back Home

Mom was so excited to hear about everything that happened in China. Over breakfast at her house, I showed her pictures of her hometown, the city of her childhood, the tombstone, the burial site, the mountains, and all of the many relatives. She was so delighted to see everything. It helped her feel part of my Chinese trip. Mom was really happy to hear how well her Chinese family was doing.

While we were talking, my sister Gloria, who had finished her morning run, came to the house to join us. She carried a black trash bag. After I finished all of my stories, she reached inside, grabbed some things, and threw them at me. To my shock and delight, they were designer handbags. I couldn't believe what I was seeing. She told me that while she was out jogging, she saw a big trash bag lying in the middle of the road. She walked over to move it out of the street and happened to see several name brand purses inside the bag.

I laughed and told Mom and Gloria about my list and how getting a designer handbag was the only thing that I didn't accomplish. But God is so faithful, he did not forget my request. Freely, he provided the handbags to me. The three of us praised God for his constant provision. Such an amazing Provider!

11

Through BSF

Through God's guidance in 2004, I joined Bible Study Fellowship International (BSF). It is a worldwide Bible Study, which tens of thousands of men and women attend. I found a weekly meeting in Moore, Oklahoma, near my home. I learned so much. Because I immersed myself in learning the English Bible, I could study with the class. I enjoyed doing the daily homework, sharing in class, listening to the lecture, and reading the lessons.

When I returned home from China, I discovered three messages on my answering machine from the BSF teaching leader. She wanted to meet me for lunch to discuss the possibility of my becoming a leader for BSF. I called her back and we made an appointment. During our lunch meeting, she said that God had told her to ask me to step into leadership at BSF and become a discussion leader. She gave me three days to pray about it and then asked me to give her an answer at the end of that time. I agreed to go to the Lord in prayer over this matter.

Entering into leadership with BSF would signify many big changes for me. Not only would it require a lot more study time; more importantly, it was definitely out of my comfort zone. As a discussion leader, I would be mentoring ten to fifteen women weekly from September to May. I worried about my English. *Would the ladies be able to understand me?* Chinese is my mother tongue, but I was raised in another world, another culture. I was so different from many of these ladies. *Would they even like me, a Chinese woman?* I struggled with self-confidence. *Who was I to be a leader?* After all, I lived many years with an abusive person. *With all of these issues, how could I bring glory to God?* I battled these concerns during my prayer time. As I sought the Lord's guidance, it became obvious to me that a change like this would help me grow deeper in my spirituality. I recalled the promise I made in the Chinese church just a few weeks earlier. I knew that this is what the Lord wanted of me. It was very clear. God gave me my answer. I was to step into the circle of BSF leadership and allow the Lord to take care of my inadequacies. He would be strong where I was weak. I prayed, "Help me to change my life. Help me to walk deeper with more commitment, with more faith, and in such a way that you will never be ashamed of me as your witness. If this call is what you really want me to do, then I will."

I called the teaching leader and told her I would become a discussion leader for BSF. It would require meeting on Tuesday mornings for leaders' training and Wednesday mornings for discussion and teaching time. Additionally, it would necessitate hours of study and preparation time for class and time to call each of my class members every week. I would have to lean on Jesus in order to be successful at making my commitment to God a reality. I wanted to serve wholeheartedly—no absences, no illnesses, and no excuses. This was a huge commitment on my part. As a piano teacher who worked with children, all kinds of diseases came in my house. I would easily catch colds from my students during the winter as they brought germs on their little fingers. I would definitely need God's special protection in order for me to fulfil this serious commitment. Great has been his faithfulness that I have not missed a class. Since stepping into leadership all of those years ago, I have been able to set aside the two mornings a week required for leadership training and to lead my group. I continue to do so to this very day.

In the beginning, leading the lessons was challenging as I learned more English. After years of learning and studying, my reading skills became fluent. I changed from speaking Chinese as my mother tongue to speaking English. The Holy Spirit guided me through the training and the leading time. I was surrounded by wonderful godly women, coworkers, and class members. I was moved and touched at each discussion session by the sharing of class members. They became my spiritual family. Every Wednesday, I was renewed. The Lord's joy filled me and washed over me just like the roaring waves of the sea.

- "He who believes in Me, as the Scripture has said, out of his heart will flow rivers of living water" (Jn. 7:38, NKJV).

What an amazing journey it has been in BSF. Each year, I am privileged to mentor and lead women deeper in the Word of God. Each year, my learning increases and my walk is more disciplined as I commit to the Lord through BSF. From the beginning, I wanted to serve God wholeheartedly. It has been glorious. Every morning, his mercies have been brand new.

12

A Christmas Miracle

My family had been celebrating Christmas in New York City, including my mother, siblings, and my sons. In 2006, my husband decided to join us so that he could spend time with his sons. By December 23, my boys arrived at Mom's home. Anticipating their father's arrival from Virginia, they were on pins and needles as they waited for him to get there. They waited and waited. He did not show up. After a while, we decided not to postpone our Christmas celebration any further since the boys' father seemed to be running a little late. As we all sat down to eat dinner, the telephone rang. The call was from the police. They notified me that my husband had been in a severe accident on highway 95. While fixing a flat tire on the side of the road, he was struck by another car. I was told that he was being rushed to the nearest emergency room with brain, stomach, and kidney bleeding. He was in critical condition. It did not sound like he would make it through the night.

I began trembling and started going into shock. Although he had been very cruel to me during the time we lived together, he was still very important to our sons. He was my boys' father. He mustn't die. He needed to live for his sons. He also needed to live so that he could meet Jesus!

"Life is in my hands," I heard the message in my heart but still I could not quit trembling. "Life is in my hands." The second time I heard it, I was able to stop shaking. I became steadier. My breathing gradually slowed. "Life is in my hands." The third time I heard the Lord whisper it to me, I understood what he was saying.

I immediately calmed down. I gathered my children together in another room and explained about the accident. They burst into loud cries of denial. Totally alarmed over the news, they were fearful of losing their father. Tears ran down their faces. As we held one another, I assured them that their father was going to be all right. "How do you know, Mom?" they asked me. I answered, "The Lord told me so. Now let's go see him."

We drove straight to the hospital. Their father was in the emergency room, barely conscious. All three of us stayed with him throughout the night. The next day, the X-rays showed great news—no more bleeding of the brain, kidneys, and stomach. Like the Lord had told me, my boys' father was going to make it. I gave him acupuncture treatment for his double vision and knee injury. In three days, he was moved out of intensive care to a regular room. In five days, he was released from the hospital to go back home. While he was hospitalized, I handled all the business details for him, such as insurance companies, car repairs, hospital expenses, and even his food. He was helpless. I felt that I was serving my Lord by helping the father of my children. It felt really gratifying to reach out and help him. Hopefully, he was able to see the Jesus in me acting kindly toward him during this time of need and helplessness. I was also willing to help him for the sake of my sons, although he still wasn't acting kind to me. In fact, he continued to upbraid me whenever I was in his presence.

I had a very busy holiday week, not at all what I had planned. Despite all the work that I was doing to help the boys' father, I was still able to return to Norman on time to begin my service to BSF for the New Year. How awesome God is! I was able to start my work as a group leader with no delays. He remembered the importance of my commitment to attend every meeting. Plus, after so much negativity thrown my way, combined with absolutely zero appreciation, I definitely needed the refreshing love of my BSF sisters.

13

Through Travel

I received a wonderful blessing in the summer of 2009. My younger sister Gladis decided to treat our mother and me to a Caribbean cruise. I had never done that before so I was really excited to be on a ship traveling to the warm waters of the Caribbean. By this time, Mom used a wheelchair almost full time. Because we were her helpers, all three of us received special consideration. If you are in a wheelchair, you and your helpers get to go to the front of every line no matter how long it is. We were allowed to board the ship first and get to sit at the front in all of the shows. It was amazing! Mom, Gladis, and I were escorted to the front every time there was a line. The staff provided excellent care. Mom never liked to trouble others, it bothered her. She also worried that she was too much work for us. Gladis told her not to give it another thought. "After all,"—she gave us a wink—"accompanying our mother gives great benefits!" We laughed.

I agreed with both of them. I never wanted to be a bother to other people. I'm more than happy to wait my turn any place, any time, but it was lovely not to wait while we were on our cruise with our wheelchair-bound mother. The three of us made wonderful memories together. I thank the Lord for blessing us with that beautiful trip. I so enjoyed our vacation. I definitely needed it because things were changing in my personal life. I was busier than I had ever been.

One major change was with my older son Brian who started working for my sister Gladis in pharmaceutical and biotechnology consulting services. Because he was bilingual, Gladis sent him to Taiwan in 2010 to work with the Taiwanese government as a validation specialist. While there, he met a sweet English teacher named Kelsie, fell in love, and proposed marriage to her. Since she lived in Taiwan, I packed my bags. I decided to travel there to meet my soon-to-be daughter-in-law. I stayed in the city of Taichung. I was so delighted to meet Kelsie. She was beautiful and seemed perfect for my Brian. It did my mother's heart a lot of good to see them so happy together. I loved spending time with them as I played tourist back in the country where I grew up. Brian served as our tour guide and showed us various sights and great restaurants. One place that I really wanted to go to was Taipei, the city of my birth. We went to Taipei 101, one of the tallest buildings in the world.

As we explored the city, seeing how things had changed since my childhood, we walked through the modern Hyatt Hotel. In the middle of its lobby were hanging two long white-striped sheets of fabric with Chinese characters written on them. Suspended four stories high, they were intended as a way to curse evil spirits and protect the residents against them. The management believed that the hotel was disturbed by many evil spirits. It was so sad. People at the Hyatt told me that before the hotel was built, this land was the center point for the execution of criminals. Many innocent people were unjustly murdered there as well. The Taiwanese believed that it was the spirits of these innocent victims that caused a lot of trouble for those who stayed in the hotel. If anyone ever had a problem while staying there, it was blamed on the spirits. If there was an accident, it was blamed on the spirits. People are very superstitious in Taiwan so they wrote curses against the evil spirits and hung the banners around as protection. It was a useless practice for two reasons. First, evil cannot get rid of evil. Mark 3:23–24, 26 says, "How can Satan drive out Satan? If a kingdom is divided against itself, that kingdom cannot stand… And if Satan opposes himself and is divided, he can not stand, his end has come." Secondly, even if evil resided in the land on which the hotel was built, the banners offered no defense. Only the Holy Spirit can cast out evil spirits. People need Jesus, not worthless written incantations that supposedly provide protection.

We returned to Taichung that evening. In the middle of the night, my bed started shaking. When I woke up feeling frightened because of the day's events, I instantly recalled 1 John 4:4, which says, "the one who lives in you is greater than he who is in the world." I refused to accept the fear that tried to take hold of me. It was no evil ghost. It was nothing but a 6.0 magnitude earthquake! It was certainly serious but not spiritual! I experienced earthquakes before as a child so I knew what to expect. I kept praying and repeating the scripture. As the safety of the Lord enveloped me, I felt his closeness throughout the rest of the night. The next day, we ended the trip with great food and enjoyed the famous night market. It was another wonderful experience spending time with my older son and his new fiancée. I had always wanted a daughter. I knew that after spending time with her, Kelsie would be a perfect addition to our family.

From Taiwan, I flew to China to visit relatives that I had not met on my previous visit. My mom's youngest sister, Little Aunt, lived in Guilin. Located near the Peach Flower River, it was the most beautiful place in China. I was able to spend time with my newly met family boating around the area, a first-time experience for me. Guilin and its surrounding countryside was simply one of the most stunning places I have ever seen. Little Aunt's family made me feel so very welcome, encouraging me to enjoy all of the scenery. A couple of days into my visit, Little Aunt told me, "I will take you to visit my dance club. It's very exclusive. Only men who have retired as high officers of the Chinese military are allowed to enter."

I did not want to go. I did not know how to dance and wasn't very motivated to meet the ladies who spent time dancing with Communist leaders. However, the Holy Spirit spoke to me that I needed to go with my Little Aunt so I went to the dance club. I was glad that I did. She introduced me to all her friends who were there. When I told them that I did not know anything about dancing, they took turns teaching me how to dance. While I was learning the various steps and moves, I shared the gospel with each lady. I asked them if the real reason they came here was to exercise in order live longer with good health. They affirmed that the reason they exercised was to live a longer life. I reminded them that we will all die eventually. Chairman Mao died and President Chiang Kai-shek died. Even though the people would say, "Long live Chairman Mao!" and "Long live President Chiang!" nonetheless they died.

I shared with the ladies that the reason the Lord God Almighty sent me to China and, ultimately, their dance club was to share with them about Jesus Christ. It is only by believing in God's Son Jesus that anyone can experience eternal life. "God loves you so much that he gave his only Son to die on a cross on your behalf. He is the one who paid the penalty for your sins. Jesus not only died for you, he also did what no other has ever done, he rose from the tomb!" I asked each lady one by one if she wanted eternal life. By the end of my dance lessons, they all accepted Jesus and were saved. They were so excited to recognize the truth from God. They asked Little Aunt if she was a Christian as well. When she answered yes, they questioned her why she had not told them of this wonderful news of Jesus Christ. As they rejoiced together in their shared Christianity, I encouraged them to go to church with Little Aunt on Sunday so that they could begin growing in their newfound faith. My visit to the beautiful city of Guilin turned out to be a beautiful time in the Lord. Praise his holy name!

I finished my Asian trip with a visit to Hong Kong. There I visited my in-laws. Hong Kong was a time of rest for me as these wonderful people welcomed me and showed me great love.

14

At a Wedding Celebration

On a Sunday afternoon back home in Oklahoma, I laid down to take a nap. Since I had several hours before my piano students would arrive, I thought I would take time for a rest, something rare for me. Just as I laid my head down on my pillow, my eyes flew open when the Lord spoke to me. He told me that I needed to get up and go shopping for my dress to wear at Brian's upcoming wedding. Obediently, I jumped out of bed and got ready to go. Since the Lord woke me up to go find a dress, I asked him where I should go shopping for it. I heard him tell me to go to the TJ Maxx store. I quickly found three beautiful dresses that I could use for the wedding in Taiwan. I needed some accessories so I asked the Lord where I should go next. "Dillard's," I heard Him direct me. At Dillard's, I found things which would fit perfectly with what I had just bought. I was so grateful. In the limited amount of free time I had, I found beautiful outfits that were perfect for my son's wedding festivities. The Lord had provided for me once again.

I showed my outfits and jewelry to one of my dear Christian sisters in BSF. She thought everything was perfect, except for one of the gold necklaces. She just didn't care for it. I agreed with her. It really didn't look all that great so she asked if she could bring some of her own jewelry for me to choose from that might work better instead. She had beautiful jewelry from which to choose. Simply gorgeous! Immediately, my eyes were drawn to a stunningly beautiful Austrian brown crystal necklace. It was very elegant and absolutely perfect for one of my new dresses. I was so honored that she lent it to me, I decided I must wear it for the first night I was in Taiwan at the wedding feast. With everything coordinated and packed for my trip, it was time for me to go.

I was excited to be back in the country of my birth for the marriage of my older son, Brian. I had already met his beautiful Kelsie, now I would meet the rest of her family. In Taiwan, the first night of the wedding celebration is a feast where the families gather to meet one another and talk about the upcoming nuptials. It was the perfect event to wear the lovely crystal necklace. On the way to the restaurant, I stopped by the fancy department store, Sogo, to do a final touch-up of my makeup. I wanted to make a good impression on Brian's new in-laws. In the ladies room as I quickly applied a coat of lipstick, the borrowed necklace suddenly broke, the beads spilling over the counter and onto the black tiled floor. They bounced and scattered everywhere. The larger beads cracked and shattered while the smaller ones rolled into every corner of the room. I was shocked! This beautiful necklace, on loan to me from my dear girlfriend from BSF had just broken apart! I started to panic because if I didn't hurry, I would be late to dinner and bring shame to my son. I frantically tried to gather all the beads I could find. What a challenge! I was thankful that I was the only one in the restroom so I could check in every corner as I picked up one small bead after another. They didn't show up well on that dark floor. Although I did the best I could, I could not be sure that I salvaged all of those that hadn't broken. My heart broke as thoroughly as the necklace. Time was running out for me to get to the dinner on time. I had to leave. I asked God for his help to stay calmed, poised, and at peace during this important dinner for my son and his fiancée. It was difficult. Only by the grace of God did my part of this special event turn out well because I was definitely preoccupied.

During dinner I had the opportunity to get to know Kelsie's family. I really liked them. Although they were very nice people, they were not believers so I knew that I must start praying for them and their salvation. When I got back at my hotel that evening, I was still feeling heartsick about the broken necklace. In spite of that, it had been a wonderful night. Brian and Kelsie were so happy. I committed myself to praying for Kelsie's family. I spent time with the Lord, asking him to move on the hearts of Brian's new family and also to help me fix my friend's necklace.

The next day, I found a jewelry store around the corner from the hotel where I was staying. When I asked the jewelers if they could fix the necklace, they told me that it would take at least three months to restring it! *How could I explain this to my friend?* Her beautiful necklace now seemed beyond repair. When my sister Gladis joined me at the hotel, I told her everything that happened the evening before. Knowing that the hotel manager was Christian, Gladis suggested that I talk to her to see if she had any ideas what I could do about the necklace. Connie, the manager, knew of a very good jeweler and suggested that I find out if this person would have time to fix it for me. She gave me the address and directions for getting there. When I got there, I discovered the address was a supply store for a Buddhist temple. I stepped in and told the owner my story about the broken necklace and then asked her if it was something she could fix. She replied, "No problem! It will be done in an hour!"

While she was working on the necklace, I felt compelled to ask her about Jesus. She told me that she had been very involved in a fellowship at a church when she was in college. She had known about Jesus but was no longer close to him since she married into a Buddhist family whose family's business was working with Buddhist temples. Sorrow crossed her face. She whispered softly that she had lost touch with Jesus for quite a while now. I shared the gospel with her. I spoke about how she only needed to repent and receive Jesus, the Son of God, into her heart, then she would be saved and have eternal life. His peace, joy, and assurance would be available to her from that moment on. Knowing she would need fellowship with other Christians, I suggested that she call Connie, the hotel manager, to help her find a strong Christian church where she could receive biblical teaching and strong Christian friends and support. She blessed me by not charging me anything for fixing the necklace. It ended up somewhat shorter, but it was nonetheless restored. I was so thankful for this miracle. So many good things came from Brian's wedding celebration. When I got home, my friend didn't care that the necklace was a smaller size. She actually liked it! Glory to God.

15

In Storm, Flood, and Love

I have lived in Tornado Alley for twenty-seven years. In Oklahoma, tornadoes are extremely common, especially in the springtime. It's the way of life. Countless tornadoes have blown through the city of Norman (where I live) and its surrounding area.

One stormy May evening, the sirens went off, warning everyone that a tornado was approaching our neighborhood. My windows rattled and my trees bent almost in half. It was frightening. I did not have a basement or a safe room so I took shelter in my closet with my Bible. I read Isaiah 4:6, "It will be a shelter and shade from the heat of the day, and a refuge and hiding place from the storm and rain." As the wind and rain raged outside, I dwelt upon his word. Such comfort in the midst of the storm! I sheltered in his protection. I was safe.

Almost a month after the storms, right before I left for New York City to visit my mother, my dear friend Janet from BSF and her father, Papa Howard, visited me. We were just talking when all of a sudden, the floor tiles in the kitchen made a weird noise and flew straight up. Never had I seen anything like that. I was so thankful that I was not alone in the house. Janet and her father witnessed it all. What was I going to do? My floor was a total wreck. I didn't know who to call or how to fix the problem. Besides, I had a plane to catch in a few days. Thankfully, Janet and Papa Howard knew people in construction who could fix my floor. Janet offered to oversee the tile repair while I was in New York so I gave her the keys to my house. She made all the arrangements. I didn't have to cancel my trip after all. The floor would be repaired while I was gone. I was so grateful.

Several weeks later while visiting Mom, I received a phone call from Janet. Her voice was very serious. She asked me if I was sitting down because if I wasn't, I needed to do so. When she said that, my heart sank. I knew it must be bad news. Janet told me that when the tile installer opened the front door of my house, he discovered that the entire first floor was flooded. Worse, there was mold everywhere. My beautiful piano, the expensive Steinway treasure from my father, had water damage down its strings. My home was destroyed, I was overwhelmed! What caused this to happen? Janet insisted that I not cut my vacation short. She assured me that she was going to call our friend Julie for help and they would start handling the problems for me.

Julie, another leader in BSF, flipped houses for a living for years. She knew construction and knew design. She discovered that the connecting hose of the washing machine in the laundry room had burst, spilling water everywhere. A plumber came to turn off the water. Julie arranged for others to remove the carpet and the moldy Sheetrock. When I came home, my house looked like a skeleton. It smelled so badly as I walked through the door, I almost fainted. With a broken heart, I called my insurance company so that I could begin the painful process of restoring my home. I wasn't sure what I was going to do and how to do it. Thankfully, I trusted that God would guide me and give me favor with all the people with whom I would come in contact. The entire process took six long heartrending months. There was so much to comprehend and figure out. First, I needed a place to stay. Finding an apartment was difficult in a university town. Even if I could find one, I would still have to buy furniture for it. It seemed like one issue after another. I felt overwhelmed. Janet's husband suggested that I move in a hotel that offered extended stays. I really liked that idea. It would make life so much easier. I prayed about it. With his guidance, I called the insurance company and they approved the plan. The hotel we agreed upon offered a fabulous breakfast every morning as well as a microwave in the room for other meals. Next, I had to take care of my students. Teaching piano was my livelihood. With my Steinway and home ruined, I had no place to teach. I called a local music store in Norman to see if they had a rental room available that I could use to teach. They told me that they were all in use until the first week of September. It was the end of August. Praise God! His timing is always perfect. The store was near my hotel, which made it very convenient for me. Plus, there was a Chinese takeout restaurant next to the store so I could grab delicious meals. I was excited by God's provision.

My friend Julie helped me with the insurance company. Although I lived in America for many years, I was still a "foreigner" when it came to dealing with insurance companies. With so much at stake, I was intimidated at times. The Lord used Julie to help me with much of the paperwork as well as cutting through the red tape of confusing bureaucracy. She found a contractor that she trusted in her flipping business. When I protested that she was doing way too much for me, she smiled and reassured me that she loved me and loved doing this kind of work. She also told me that whatever I needed, she would take care of. She wanted to help and she wanted to minister to my needs. Help and minister she did. She funneled God's love to me in this very trying time and provided great practical, spiritual, and emotional support. Julie was a special blessing. I guess insurance companies have so many hoops for claimants to jump through because there are those who try to take advantage. Nonetheless, it can be difficult for an honest naïve person like me who is trying to get things taken care of. I would call, get an answering machine, leave a message, and wait for a call back. When no one called me back, I would call once more, get the answering machine again, leave another message, and continue to wait for a call back. This happened day after day. It was almost laughable how it was so routine. The Lord reminded me of the following scripture from Proverbs 16:33, which says, "The lot is cast into the lap, but every decision is from the Lord." His word gave me hope and strength to handle the problem of the insurance company when I was ready to give up.

Early in the process of repairing my home, I went to the scene of the crime, the laundry room. Contractors were tearing out some paneling that only contained dead space next to a closet. While they were working, the Lord conveyed to me that this space should be used for a refuge against any storms. "Ask the contractors to make it into a tornado shelter for you. I would not have you afraid during storm season ever again. Make it big enough for you and any students you might have in your home at the time. Go to the contractors and tell them now," he said to me. The contractors agreed completely with this plan. It was an easy fix. Now I would have a safe place in my house to go to when the tornado sirens sounded a warning to my neighborhood. Remembering the verse in Isaiah that I had meditated on during the last tornado, I smiled as I realized that I had a refuge from storms. The Lord had provided me a sanctuary. This was one of many times I saw the Lord's hand move on my behalf during the restoration of my home. Not only did I have a temporary place to live, a space to teach, and a God-directed safe room, the insurance company finally decided to replace my beautiful grand piano, the most expensive thing I owned. I serve a mighty God. He was not satisfied with just taking care of a few minor things here and there. My Lord God was constantly at work improving things for my home. He gave me countless miracles one after another that not only included the new safe room, but also new windows, floor, blinds, paint, and lighting. He blessed me as he overcame challenge after challenge.

The windows in my house are very tall. My beautiful double-paned windows were clouded with heavy mist from the flooding. The insurance company refused to replace them even though they were clearly impacted by all of the water in my house. The damage was awful. The fogged up windows made my house look like something out of a Halloween horror show. There was no feeling of peace or tranquility when I tried to see out of them. In fact, the opposite was true. They gave off a bad feeling. Workers shuddered when they entered the house and saw them. That was definitely not the atmosphere I desired for my home. I wanted my visitors to feel peaceful when they walked through the door rather than wrestling with ambivalent emotions of unrest and unease. After spending time in prayer, I asked a dear friend for advice. She suggested that if it was affordable, I should replace all of the windows and pay for them myself before I moved back in. It made sense because I decided the windows would continue to bother me from now on. I agreed to obtain some quotes. The first company I approached gave me a bid of ten thousand dollars, which was way too high for me. I did not have that kind of money available. As the insurance adjuster already told me that the company would not pay to change out the damaged windows, I just didn't know what to do. With a conflicted heart, I went to the Lord, seeking his wisdom. A mother of one of my students gave me the name of a company she used. They worked up an estimate of seven thousand dollars. Meanwhile, during the midst of this entire renovation, various insurance adjusters were assigned to my case one after another. They kept changing. There were times I had no idea with whom I was supposed to speak to get my questions answered. Following God's guidance, I decided to go ahead and order the lower-priced windows. It really was not an option. I needed them. I also believed in my heart that the Lord directed me to purchase them. Trusting that the he would help me pay for them, even if it was one window at a time, I would have all of them replaced. The feel of the house immediately changed with the beautiful new windows.

Afterward, I heard the Holy Spirit tell me to send in the invoice for the cost of the window replacement. I thought, *No, the first adjuster adamantly told me no way would the insurance company pay for those windows.* I wasn't going to embarrass myself and look foolish while getting my claim rejected! I already knew their answer. Once more, the Holy Spirit told me to turn in the invoice. Again, I said no. A third time, I heard his command, "Turn it in." Finally, I was obedient. Taking a deep breath, I faxed it in and promptly forgot all about it. I had zero expectation for a reimbursement payment. My Lord, however, had other plans. Days later, I received a letter from the insurance company. When I opened the envelope, I saw that it was a check from the insurance company and quickly took it to my bank to deposit it. I never even looked at the amount. I just endorsed it and deposited it. When I received my monthly bank statement, the Holy Spirit told me to verify the deposit on my bank statement. I obeyed. There in the deposit column, I saw the amount exactly matched the invoice for the cost of the windows. I had been totally reimbursed! God was so patient with me although I had resisted his voice. He wanted to bless me even when I thought it was impossible. Praise the Lord!

During this time of reconstruction, I did not like to go back to my home because it was really difficult to see the reality of such destruction. It hurt my heart. This house had been my refuge. Furthermore, it was also my place of business. It was where I had taught each one of my piano students for the past twenty-seven years. It was painful to reconcile my memories with the stark reality of the desolation. One day, I heard the Lord tell me to go to my house. I did so. When I arrived, the workman who was going to install the blinds was there taking measurements. He recommended that I upgrade to a better quality of blinds. He thought that for the difference in price, the better blinds would last longer and look much nicer. The cost would be less than five hundred bucks so I had him change my work order. I gave thanks to God. The installer was absolutely correct, the blinds perfectly complemented the wooden floor that was later installed!

The renovation had been going on in my house for four long months. It was time for the Christmas holidays and time for my annual trip to see Mom in New York. Although I usually fly early in the morning when I go to New York, this time I could only get reservations for late afternoon. Since I would be gone for two weeks spending time with my family out of state, the painter volunteered to work on the house while I was away. I picked out a golden hue that I thought would be nice. The walls would be done by the time I returned in January. The painter showed up the morning of the day of my departure to give me a chance to preview my color choice. It looked dreadful on the wall! It wouldn't work at all. I breathed a prayer of thanks to God that he had given me this opportunity to see what the paint color would look like. Because my plane did not leave until later, I had plenty of time to change the paint to a pearl white, which I absolutely loved. God had sovereignly arranged my schedule. A painting disaster was avoided!

The dining area in my house had always been a dark room. When the electrician came, I asked him to put a new light above the formal dining table. He asked the insurance company about it and received permission to add one additional light fixture. He told me that if I could purchase it before the end of the week, he would install it himself right away. One of my BSF friends, Mary Helen, gave me a gift card to spend on the house. I took it to the lighting shop. The fixture with three lights was sold out. There was no time to place a back order so I added the money from the gift card to get a four-light chandelier. I was going to have light for the first time in the dining room. I was so happy! When the light fixture was installed, it was beautiful and bright. The whole room lit up. But when I counted, there were five lights, not the four I had ordered. I give thanks to God. He knew exactly how many light bulbs I needed. The room was absolutely perfect.

I had a very hard time choosing the right flooring. There were just so many varieties to choose from, so many colors, and so many styles that I was completely confused. I didn't know what to do. I asked my friend Julie who knew a lot about flooring. She told me the bigger the tile, the less impact the grout would have on the ambience of the room. With her help, I selected a style that would work well in my house. By the time of the Chinese New Year in February 2014, the floor was finally finished. With that, the house was completely renovated. I could move back home now. With a deep breath of quiet rejoicing, I gave thanks to God. The Lord clearly used this catastrophic flood in my life and turned it into something extraordinarily beautiful. He turned devastation into victory. My God provided a modern kitchen for me with new countertops, cabinets, flooring, and windows all paid for by the insurance company. My home was more beautiful than before the disaster.

I decided not to use my brand new Steinway & Sons grand piano for teaching lessons but keep it for performance use only. Since I needed an upright piano, I bought a Kimball from a church member. Then one of my BSF sisters gave me her Baldwin piano. At the very same time, a dear sister in Christ needed a piano for her two children taking piano lessons. I was able to pass a piano on to them. In beautiful symmetry, God provided one for them as well as one for me with which to teach my students. What an abundance of blessing! When we obey God, there is plenty for everyone.

Through this process, I discovered that my friends deeply loved me. They supported me every step of this painful process. During the ordeals of life, I have always been the strong one, helping others during their season of need. However, in this experience, the shoe was on the other foot. I was humbled by their unconditional love and servant's heart as my friends ministered to me during my personal disaster. Along with God, they kept me encouraged and strong. I give all the praise to the Lord Most High. Only he could clearly turn disaster into victory in so many ways.

16

During Loss

During Christmas of 2014, we all gathered together as usual at Mom's home in New York City. My heart was heavy because I knew the moment was drawing near for her to go to her heavenly home. It was clear to all of us. Thankfully, the Lord had prepared me. During my Bible study of Deuteronomy, I contemplated the life of Moses. Although he was a faithful servant of the Lord and the Israelites needed him, Moses was called home. God's word opened my heart and mind.

I spent most of the holidays holding my mother's hand and praying for her. Most of that time, her eyes were closed. As I sat next to her, I thought about her life. Mom had been the pillar of our family since my dad passed away thirty-five years earlier. Her entire life, she loved Jesus. Mom was a kind person. Even as a child, she would bring classmates cookies and cared about the people around her. She was also extremely intelligent, having been raised by sharp business people. These characteristics were passed on to her beloved family.

Meanwhile, my younger son Hamilton joined me in New York. He was excited because he had just been offered a new position on Wall Street. He wanted my help in finding him an apartment close to his new job. Hamilton narrowed it down to three choices. His favorite was only a block from his workplace, he could simply walk there whenever he needed. I told him that I would be happy to look at this apartment with him and set an appointment to see it in the afternoon. Before then, I went to the corner store and brought egg custard back home for Mom to enjoy. The home attendant had no idea that I was coming back to feed my mother before I left to go apartment hunting with Hamilton. The woman was enraged as she jumped in front of my mom's bed and began yelling at me to get out of the room. I was shocked! My mother's eyes opened from all the commotion. She looked at me with her beautiful dark eyes that told me she understood my confusion. I discovered that my sweet dying mom had the same experience from this attendant. I refused to fear this woman as she threw her fit. I told Mom, "It is almost 2015, and we can thank God for his continual protection." There were some changes I would make regarding her care now that I realized what was going on. When the doorbell rang, I opened the door to Hamilton. He was ready to take me to see his prospective apartment. I turned back to Mom's room to tell her that I was stepping out for a little bit, but the attendant already locked her door! She refused to let me in because my mom was supposedly resting. In the interest of keeping the peace, I did not argue but told her I would be back soon. Then I left with my son. Hamilton decided the apartment was perfect for him as it was within a couple of blocks of his new job downtown. I praised the Lord as Hamilton signed the lease because he had given my son his heart's desire for a great location.

Things happened quickly in those few days. Hamilton moved into his new place and I was able to say goodbye to my precious mother. After the holidays, I flew back to Oklahoma on Thursday, January 1, 2015. I felt very satisfied with my Christmas visit. Knowing that she would be leaving soon for her heavenly home, I understood that I might be returning to New York before too long, although I did not know how I could possibly do so. Airfare was very expensive. I also had my BSF responsibility. Two days later on a Saturday morning, Mom peacefully left this earth to go be with the heavenly Father in our eternal home.

While I rejoiced for Mom who was one of the godliest people I knew, I felt some grief for myself. I did not know how I was going to be able to afford a ticket back to New York on such short notice. My family initially decided to have Mom's service on Wednesday. I was concerned about this. Besides not being able to afford the airfare, I made a commitment to God about my Wednesday BSF attendance, I would never miss a class. Since we had been out for Christmas Break, it was time for BSF to resume. What was I going to do? How could I make it all work together? There's only one way in a situation like this—pray and let God handle it.

The first miracle came with a phone call from one of my sisters. The family reconsidered and determined that having Mom's service on Wednesday was too soon for all of the relatives who had to make the trip to New York. My sisters decided to move the day of the funeral and hold it on a Friday instead. I smiled at the news. I would still be able to lead my BSF group and not miss class! Another miracle happened when one of my dear BSF sisters told me that the Lord spoke to her about providing me a standby airplane ticket. God was still in control! After leading Wednesday's Bible study, I flew from Oklahoma City to Dallas to catch a plane to New York. However, when I arrived in Dallas/Fort Worth International Airport, the plane to New York was full so there was no room for me. Flying on standby meant that I couldn't have a reserved seat. I thought about changing my destination to Philadelphia. My older son Brian, who now lived in Pennsylvania, could pick me up there and drive me to New York. I discussed this possibility with the airline agent. She was very sympathetic knowing that I was traveling to attend my mother's funeral. She asked me to wait a moment as she looked at schedules on her computer. With a smile, she told me that she had discovered a flight connecting from Houston to LaGuardia Airport and there were at least seventy-five seats available! She booked me from Dallas to Houston to New York. It was such a miracle as God worked out my travel plans using this caring airline employee. He put it all together for me, step by step. I arrived in New York late that evening. Gladis picked me up without delay. I felt God's caring heart during this emotional time.

The day of Mom's funeral was a beautiful snowy Friday. Mom loved the snow. Each time it snowed, my mother rejoiced and thanked God for it. She just found it so lovely. Many of Mom's old friends came from California to pay their respects to her. Being from

Southern California, they had never seen so much snow. They were so excited to experience it that they even took selfies of themselves in the snow. My mother would have laughed at their enjoyment. The entire cemetery was covered in the thick white snow. Although it was a very solemn occasion, I had never seen such a beautiful sight. I normally did not like visiting the cemetery, even though my father was buried there as well. But on that day, I could clearly see the hand of God in this entire situation as we celebrated Mom's life of serving the Most High. Everything was pure, clean, and white.

Suddenly, the sun came out, and it shone on her coffin as they began to lower it. Brightness took away the darkness of the burial site. The Lord spoke to me from Isaiah 1:18, "Though your sins are like scarlet, they shall be as white as snow; though they are red as crimson, they shall become like wool." In a cold January day, his words comforted me and warmed my heart. When we believe in Jesus, as my mother did, he takes away our sins forever and covers us with his love.

The news of my mother's death had been extremely painful to my younger sister, Gladis. That particular weekend, she was flying back from a business trip in Asia. She was out of the country working rather than visiting with Mom, as she normally did on a Saturday. For the past ten years, she had devoted almost every weekend to our mother. Mom and her home health care attendants called Gladis "Santa Claus" for all the gifts she brought each week. She took care of Mom's needs. Mom really looked forward to her weekly visits. On the Saturday of Mom's death, Gladis made it back in New York that afternoon. To my sister's deepest dismay, our mom was already gone. She passed away just hours before Gladis arrived so she was unable to say goodbye. She mourned with an overwhelming grief. With her heart broken, my siblings and I could not comfort her. Only our heavenly Father could. The day after the funeral, Mom appeared to my sister. God swept Gladis' tears away and comforted her in a very unique way. Praise him for his kindness!

While my brothers and sisters were saddened by our loss, we still had joy and peace. Mom, though absent from her body, was alive with the Lord. My siblings and I were able to rejoice in the midst of our loss because of John 11:25–26, "Jesus said to her, 'I am the resurrection and the life. The one who believes in me will live, even though they die; and whoever lives by believing in me will never die.'"

17

Allowing Him to Work amid My Injury

After Mom went home to be with the Lord, Gladis invited me to spend part of the summer with her. It was a great idea! We both could use the special bonding time at her house in New Jersey. We decided to spend a couple of weeks in New Jersey and then travel to Pennsylvania to spend time with Brian and Kelsie. Our visit would coincide with a visit from his in-laws. Kelsie's mother and sister-in-law with her two children were coming from Taiwan for their second visit to America. On their first visit, they stayed with my mother and had been exposed to Christian thinking and music. This time around, the children were attending an American summer camp and would be staying with Brian and Kelsie. My sister and I had been praying for Brian's new family since the wedding in Taiwan. Although wonderful and kind people, they still did not know Jesus. I was looking forward to spending time with them and sharing about the great love that the Lord had for them. With the Lord's leading, I knew that it was the right season for Brian's in-laws to understand the great love of our Lord Jesus.

So six months later in June, after BSF entered into its summer hiatus, I arrived in New Jersey. While disembarking from the plane, my right knee collapsed. Crying aloud in pain, I stumbled my way out of the airplane then found myself in such severe agony that I could not even walk! The airport provided me a wheelchair to get around the terminal and to go to Gladis' car. This was definitely an opportunity to seek God's help. I had no other choice. Crippling pain kept me housebound while I was at my sister's house. Day after day, with faith and prayer, I performed acupuncture on my knee. This knee pain ran deeply and refused to relinquish its grasp on my knee. Basically crippled and incapacitated, my sister had to take care of me. While trying to work through the pain, I was aware that our time to spend with Brian and his in-laws was running out. How could I minister to his in-laws when I was so immobile? Finally, Gladis said that we should go visit Brian while his in-laws were still there. I agreed. I realized that no matter how bad the pain in my injured knee was, I could not allow it to keep me from my mission to share the gospel of God's great love.

Arriving at Brian's home, we were welcomed with wonderful hospitality. Because my knee had delayed our coming to Pennsylvania, I refused to waste even one minute of valuable time. With Gladis praying quietly in the background, I began teaching about Jesus and his salvation with everyone there. I could clearly feel the presence of the Most High as he filled the room with his love and gentleness. Brian's new family was very open to hear about Jesus. Then very quietly, the Holy Spirit told me that it was time to take a pause, reflect for a moment, and discuss other things for a time. So I did. I then prayed and asked God when I should resume sharing about his great love again. I really wanted to lead these special people to Christ. The Lord told me to wait a little while longer. When everyone decided to go shopping at the outlet mall, I decided to join them even though my knee was still not yet recovered. We walked from store to store. I continued to pray asking God when it would be the right moment, but the outlet mall was not the right place for a conversation about eternity.

Gladis and I were invited to share tea with them when we returned to Brian's house. As we sipped from our cups, Gladis disclosed, "My mother had us pray before each meal. We were brought up giving thanks to God before eating." She went on to describe how our mother taught the six of us children how to pray, read, and memorize Bible verses. The younger child, Ashley, did not understand exactly what we were talking about. She was only five years old. I remembered that she learned the song "Jesus Loves Me" when she visited us in America two years earlier so I sang the song and she joined in! She understood salvation immediately after that. I knew that now was the time to begin sharing once more. I told them about the great love that the Lord has for us. It was so great that he sent his only Son (Jesus) to pay the price for our sins. When I was finished, all of Brian's in-laws, including little Ashley, prayed the prayer of salvation and were saved! God is so faithful. I encouraged them to find a church to attend when they returned to Taiwan. All agreed to do so. They were excited to become active in their Taipei church and share the good news about Jesus with all who attended there.

My sister and I drove back to her home in Jersey, praising God all the way. When we entered her living room, I received a phone call from Brian. He said, "Mom, guess what happened? Tonight, before we started eating dinner, Ashley reminded us that we had not yet prayed and given thanks to God for our food." So Brian led all of them in a thankful blessing for their meal. What a beautiful testimony! God can use a five-year-old child to remind an entire family to give thanks to God for what He has provided! Truly, God answered my prayers for these wonderful people. The devil attacked my knee to keep me from sharing the good news but Jesus still won the battle! Through this experience, I was reminded that we were fighting a spiritual war. We would have many roadblocks that we must press through and never give up.

As the summer came to a close, I flew home to Oklahoma with a heart full of joy and with a cane to help me walk. God had his way! After continued prayer and more acupuncture, my knee recovered fully.

18

Despite Physical Pain

BSF was coming to a close for another year. It was May 2016, I was making preparations to attend the wedding of my nephew Daniel, Gladis' son. In just one more week, I would have finished my service and obligations to BSF. I then would catch a plane for Irvine, California, to attend all of the wedding festivities. I was filled with joy for Daniel and his new bride.

While enjoying the late spring sunshine in my yard, my body suddenly seized up from the pain of a severe toothache. My hands flew up to cradle the throbbing side of my face. It really hurt! How could such a small thing as a tooth cause so much pain? I was grateful that it hadn't begin hurting while I was at BSF. Leading the study of the last chapter of Revelations had taken my full concentration. Now this toothache demanded all of my attention.

I made an emergency appointment with my dentist and rushed to see her. During the examination, she told me that one of my teeth under the bridge in my mouth had decayed. Not only would she have to replace the bridge, she would also have to do a root canal on the throbbing tooth. This was going to be extremely expensive to fix. My heart sank at the news. I did not have time for a medical emergency. I wanted to go celebrate my nephew's joy with my family. Such bad news! But it got worse. The bottom of the bridge was chipped. So each time I ate, bits of food would get caught under the bridge, causing more problems. Eating developed into a painful ordeal. The doctor told me that this tooth would have to be pulled. The estimate for this problem and the root canal on the other tooth that needed a crown totaled nearly four thousand dollars. Disheartened and overwhelmed with pain, I went to the Lord to pray about these issues. After a time, I felt him lead me to seek a second opinion. So I went to see another dentist. This dentist disagreed with the treatment plan of the first dentist. This specialist told me that by using an implant post, he could save my tooth. Plus, his dental work came in at only two thousand five hundred. I was happy to hear that I would be able keep my tooth and the cost would be significantly lower than the first estimate. I decided to book an appointment and get everything fixed with the second dentist. The work was scheduled in late August after all the celebrations and summer family visits were over. When the wedding festivities concluded, I flew to New Jersey to spend time with my sister.

At her church, I ran into an old friend of ours who was a dentist. He was suffering from severe shoulder pain and required my immediate help. Interested in alternative medicine, he asked about my acupuncture skills and experience. I discovered that his pain was caused by the overuse of his hands and poor posture while working with patients in his dental practice. After I performed several sessions of acupuncture treatments, Gladis asked him to please look at my dental problems because I was miserably in pain from my tooth. He offered to meet me the next day in his office. His rapid willingness took me completely by surprise. I didn't even have my X-rays with me because I didn't think that I needed them before my appointment in Oklahoma in eight days. My plan was just to endure the pain until I could get back home and then have it fixed. But this dentist insisted upon helping me. He saved the decayed tooth, confirming the second dentist's prediction that it was possible. As for the bridge and crown, it would take a full week to get them done. I really didn't want to change my return flights to meet his schedule because I needed to be back in Oklahoma for the BSF kickoff. If I changed my flight, then I would miss my class, compromising my promise to God. The Lord whispered in my ear, "Ask if the work can be done a little quicker." When I asked him, the dentist replied that he could repair everything, including the crown and bridgework, in four days if we met on the weekend.

We were so excited. It was a perfect example of God's special miracles, providing relief from pain in our bodies. Meanwhile, I decided to make the most of my time in the Northeast, enjoying my family before all of this dental work started. I made a trip to Pennsylvania to visit Brian and Kelsie. My son cooked a delicious steak for me. It was so tender that I could chew it despite my painful teeth. The lobster was also cooked perfectly. I had no problem eating my entire meal. Next, I went to Gladis' house in New Jersey. The two of us visited Mom's grave. I reflected on the legacy she left for me, a legacy of service, piano skill, and a deep love for our heavenly Father. I appreciated the training she gave me as a young child, which set the groundwork for my adult faith and ministry.

Grace joined us for lunch. She was suffering from agonizing pain in her leg. She was even considering canceling our family dinner because her leg pain was preventing her from walking. With my needles, I began working on her with a session of acupuncture. Grace made so much progress in an hour that not only did she make it to dinner, she was even able to walk me to the elevator. Praise God for his healing mercies.

The next day, I made arrangements with Hamilton to eat *dim sum* in Chinatown. After we finished our meal, he showed me how he had fixed up his apartment. It was so good for a mother's heart to see how happy he was. Afterward, he walked me to the bus station so that I could get back to Gladis' house in time for my dentist appointment. It worked out perfectly. There was enough time for the doctor to fit a bridge and crown for me. It was all done. It was the perfect cost as well. Because it was a little over half of the previous estimates, I was able to pay cash to have my teeth fixed. Praise God!

That summer had been amazing. Besides getting my teeth fixed at a much reduced rate and attending my nephew's wedding, I had the opportunity to attend my daughter-in-law Kelsie's U.S. citizenship naturalization ceremony. I was so happy for her and just kept repeating my congratulations. She was now my very dear "American" daughter-in-law! Recently, she became the mother of my first grandchild, Hannah. After years of praying, God blessed us all with little Hannah. She was an answer to a grandmother's prayers. *Hallelujah!* My heart was full of thanks to God. Proverbs 16:9 states that, "In their hearts humans plan their course, but the Lord establishes their steps." Amen and amen!

19

Now and Forever

It is my prayer that you too experience the living God in every area of your life. Let me encourage you not to hold on to things yourself. Give them to God. He can amply and abundantly take care of you and the situations you face. What may look like disaster can evolve into something beautiful, exceeding your expectations. Clearly, as you have seen from my life, he has turned ashes into beauty. Just as I do, you can completely trust our heavenly Father.

My marriage is still a very painful area in my life, but I wanted to be transparent with you and let you know that I still pray for my boys' father. Like all of us, he needs Jesus. For these past decades since I have committed all that I am to Jesus the Christ, I have purposefully sat at his feet through prayer, Bible reading, and meditating on his word each and every day. I am a renewed and well-loved person. The Lord has rebuilt my self-esteem. Lifting me up in leadership as a confident woman, he has equipped me to serve and love my community. I have served as the music director of my church, taught Sunday school, chaired the mission committee, and served as a pianist for the Southern Oklahoma Chinese Baptist Church (SOCBC) for church worship and fellowships. From a beaten-down, worthless woman, the Lord transformed me into a happy, confident, and strong Christian with purpose. No longer do I hang my head in fear, shame, and despair. Through God's love, I carry myself as an heir of the Most High. What the Lord did for me, he will do for anyone.

There was a time when death and despair overwhelmed me. I was beaten down. I discovered that the Lord proved to be stronger than any of the obstacles that I encountered in my life.

God has a purpose for each of his children. Philippians 2:13 (English Standard Version) says, "For it is God who works in you, both to will and to work for his good pleasure." All you have to do is to repent and totally surrender your life to our Lord Jesus. He will help you live life to the fullest with great joy. If you are interested in a deeper walk with God's word in a loving environment, visit the website for BSF (www.bsfinternational.org) and get further information. It is an exciting adventure of biblical truth and study for women and men all over the world. BSF enables you to "see the goodness of God" with people who love him. Experience the living God and experience life, purpose, and joy. God bless you!

If you desire to develop a relationship with God, then please stop where you are and pray, "God, I understand that I am a sinner. I want you to please forgive me of my sins. I ask that you take over my heart and my life. I accept Jesus as the Savior and Lord of my life. Jesus, thank you for your salvation. Thank you for my new life."

Call or visit a Bible-based church and let the pastor know that you have just accepted Jesus in your heart. Your local church will help you on your new and exciting walk with the Lord God Almighty. If possible, get involved with a local BSF group. They can be found everywhere. Visit the BSF website to find a group near you. Let me know so that I can also pray for you. Bless you!

體驗永生的神，體驗生命、目的和喜樂 願主保佑你

About the Author

Lily was born in Taiwan in a God-loving home. She has five siblings, two brothers and three sisters. Lily's mother trained all six of her children according to Deuteronomy 11:19, "Teach them to your children, talking about them when you sit at home and when you walk along the road, when you lie down and when you get up." Lily was baptized at age twelve. But at age six, she started learning to play the piano under her mother's strict discipline.

In 1974, she came to the United States of America to study at Florida State University where she received a master of music education degree. In 1978, Lily received her second master's degree, this one is in piano performance, from Brooklyn College in New York City. In 1990, a crisis happened in her life, which became a turning point for her to return to God. In 2006, while she was visiting her hometown church in China, God revealed to Lily that she was a lukewarm Christian. It was a wake-up call that she needed to change the life she used to live. She stepped out of her comfort zone by answering God's calling to serve in Bible Study Fellowship International as a discussion leader. She has already done this for more than thirteen years. Lily started serving in her church as a pianist at the age of fifteen while she was in Taiwan. She taught Sunday school for twelve years at her home church, Southern Oklahoma Chinese Baptist Church (SOCBC). She has also served as the choir director, the chairperson of the mission department, and the pianist for the Sunday worship service.

John 10:10 (ESV) says, "I came that they may have life and have it abundantly." Walking with Jesus, Lily tasted the goodness of his promised abundant life. Jude 1:21 (ESV) says, "Keep yourself in the love of God, waiting for the mercy of our Lord Jesus Christ that leads to eternal life." This is the motto of Lily's present daily life. Praise God! The love of the Lord never ceases, his mercy never comes to an end.

CPSIA information can be obtained
at www.ICGtesting.com
Printed in the USA
FFHW021957281019
55841977-61710FF